THE INTELLIGENT GOLFER

GOLFER

How to Play a Civilized Game

THE INTELLIGENT GOLFER

How to Play a Civilized Game

THE ESSENTIAL GUIDE TO SUCCEEDING ON THE WORLD'S FINEST COURSES

BY SCOTT MARTIN

UNIVERSE

To Andrew

Published by Universe Publishing
A Division of Rizzoli International Publications, Inc.
300 Park Avenue South
New York, NY 10010
www.rizzoliusa.com

Project Editor: Candice Fehrman
Book Design: Lori S. Malkin
Line Art: © Christopher King / Dreamstime.com

2011 2012 2013 2014 / 10 9 8 7 6 5 4 3 2 1

Printed in China

ISBN-13: 978-0-7893-2219-7

Library of Congress Catalog Control Number:
2010933492

CONTENTS

ACKNOWLEDGMENTS

Author and publisher Bryan Curtis created an extremely successful series about manners and I am grateful he decided to start a new series, *The Intelligent Sportsman*. I am honored he invited me to write the first book in the series.

James Fawcett helped me refine my typing skills several years ago and I will always be in his debt.

Andrew Wood and everyone at Legendary Marketing in Lecanto, Florida, are wonderful people and have helped me develop a new skill set and a new approach to writing—an approach I'm enjoying hugely.

Charles Hipp calls me The Lama. Why? Because I can't hit the ball out of my shadow. Cheers!

Thank you to all the golf professionals who work so hard to make golf the greatest of all games. Without you, we'd all be playing darts, or pool, or standing by a slot machine somewhere.

INTRODUCTION

Let me introduce you to a gentleman named Nigel Denham, not perhaps the most famous golfer of all time, but nonetheless a better-than-decent player who competed in the 1974 English Amateur Strokeplay Championship at Moortown Golf Club in Leeds, a bustling city in northern England. Near the conclusion of his round, Denham struck his approach shot to the eighteenth green, only to watch in amazement as his ball went over the green, landed on a path in front of the clubhouse, clambered up some steps, entered an open door, and pinballed to its final resting spot in the *bar*, which, at the time, was populated with several members who had been enjoying a full afternoon of refreshment and banter.

As Leeds can be a somewhat muddy place, even in a biblical drought, golfers at Moortown must change their shoes before entering certain parts of the clubhouse, including the bar. So Denham dutifully removed his golf shoes and entered the fray to assess the situation. The clubhouse was not out of bounds. Fortunately, Denham discovered that he had a clear shot to the green, albeit through a window, and simply followed the most important rule of all: play the ball as it lies. He had to move some furniture and ask the members to relocate their libations momentarily. Denham selected a club from his bag, opened the window, and hit a fine shot that ended up a mere twelve feet from the hole, much to the amazement of the members, who expressed their admiration for the achievement.

Similar situations are, of course, extremely rare. They are so rare that Denham's initial plight and subsequent recovery created a great deal of headscratching among the people who interpret the rules of golf in the United Kingdom, specifically a group of rules experts in the clubhouse of the Royal and Ancient Golf Club in St. Andrews, Scotland. Golf has a set of official rules that fit neatly into a small pocket-sized booklet appropriately titled *The Rules of Golf*. However, the accompanying tome, *Decisions on the Rules of Golf*, weighs 1.3 pounds and has 670 pages. This proves that while golf can sometimes seem like an easy game to understand, the written rules are usually mysterious, indecipherable, occluded, baffling, foggy, and bizarre.

Thankfully, and ironically, golf's *unwritten* rules are easier to understand. Many people who take up golf leave the game shortly after their first forays because they feel intimidated, clumsy, and very much on the outside looking in, most often because their knowledge of basic etiquette is sparse, which is a pity. As Dana Rader, the founder of the Dana Rader Golf School in Charlotte, North Carolina, says, the goal of every golfer and everyone in golf should be to grow the game. So this book represents my way of making that happen by helping you feel at ease with the game, its people, and its surroundings so that you feel confident and comfortable wherever you happen to find yourself in the golf universe.

I hope, in fact, that you find yourself at one of the carefully chosen golf destinations detailed in this book. Here you will find inside information about places such as Pinehurst, Pebble Beach, St. Andrews, and the superb Bandon Dunes on the wild Oregon coast. It is the duty and responsibility of every golfer to visit one of these shrines at least once in his or her life—anyone can play them, given the time and inclination. But this book also features numerous less-famous spots that should be on your radar soon, if not right away. Whether you are on the eighteenth tee at Pebble Beach or the first tee at Machrihanish in Scotland, the site of the top opening hole on the planet, you will, after reading and digesting this book, feel like you are part of the golfing world so that golf is what it should always be: civilized without being pompous, and hugely enjoyable without being technically demanding.

This book answers numerous golf questions and will help you navigate through the golf etiquette maze. If your boss invites you to play at his or her club, where should you change your shoes? If a client asks you to attend a golf tournament, what should you wear and how should your spouse dress? Is it appropriate, at said event, to yell "You da man!" when a professional is putting? What should you do if you are at a club and the person with whom you are playing asks you to concede a four-foot putt on the eighteenth green? Perhaps you are thinking about a golf trip to Scotland and don't know where to start (or finish). Maybe you have been avoiding playing golf with someone important in your business life because you are worried about basic golf manners. Don't worry. This book is here to help you find the great places to play and to help you enjoy them. It's also here to help you feel at ease whether you are standing on the first tee at Pine Valley, usually considered the world's top golf course, or visiting the Masters for the first time.

Golf is not an easy game. All the top golfers (Ben Hogan, Tiger Woods, Nick Faldo, Danny Noonan, Arnold Palmer, etc.) have had one thing in common: the pulsating and almost obsessive desire to improve and turn a 67 into a 66 or 65. It's impossible to conquer golf, yet the truly intelligent golfer understands that it *is* possible to enjoy the game, given the right expectations, approach, and attitude. The intelligent golfer understands that golf is much more than the number of shots taken over eighteen holes or the result of the match.

The intelligent golfer seeks the finest places to play. The intelligent golfer understands the game's etiquette but is not despotic about the unwritten rules. The intelligent golfer relishes meeting new golfers and making even more golfing friends. The intelligent golfer plans ahead and researches the next golf destination on the agenda but is always willing and able to take an "emergency" golf trip. The intelligent golfer may not have the time or natural ability to become good enough to compete in amateur or professional tournaments but takes enough quality instruction to be competent enough to play anywhere. The intelligent golfer enjoys golf destinations where golf is more important than creed, color, gender, or political affiliation. The intelligent golfer feels comfortable anywhere in golf and always helps newcomers to the game feel the same way. The intelligent golfer knows at least three (clean) golf jokes and a few of the key lines from *Caddyshack*. The intelligent golfer has read at least one book about golf history and knows that it was Gene Sarazen who hit "the shot heard around the world" on his way to winning the Masters in 1935. And, perhaps most important, the intelligent golfer knows how to react and the requisite course of action should his or her approach shot to the eighteenth green end up in the member's bar.

My express wish is that *The Intelligent Golfer* gets you more excited about golf and more fired up to visit its top destinations than ever before. Golf is, and always should be, an adventure. My complementary wish is that the book helps you feel comfortable with the game, even if you are playing the fifteenth hole on the Old Course at St. Andrews, the wind is blowing at forty miles per hour, and the sharp rain is coming in horizontally. Armed with the knowledge in this book, you will at least know about a couple of spots in the town where you will find appropriate shelter and ample refreshment to aid your recovery from exposure to the sometimes cruel Scottish elements. And you will also know that, as an intelligent golfer, you always buy the first round if you win the match.

EPIC GOLF DESTINATIONS

Golf provides the perfect excuse for a well-deserved vacation and the perfect reason to plan an adventure to a beautiful place where a group of people, for whatever reason, decided to create, devise, develop, and build a place dedicated purely to pampering, ease, relaxation, and the maximum enjoyment of the greatest game. In common golf parlance, such a place is known as a "golf resort," but that's a hugely pedestrian phrase that fails to describe what makes a golf destination so special. The writer who came up with "golf resort" was clearly *not* a golfer and wasn't much of a writer either.

North America alone has more than 100 golf resorts and destinations. They come in all shapes and sizes, from the international mega-destination to the regional favorite. At each golf destination, whatever the size and scope, the people who make these places tick spend untold energy ensuring that every guest and visitor is giddy from the moment they arrive to the moment they leave. The much-decorated chef wants to make absolutely certain that your steak is cooked just the way you like it. The person who cuts the greens every morning wants you to make all your short putts. The shoeshine expert wants you to see the reflection of the full moon in your Bostonians when you walk from the lobby to the restaurant. The sommelier in the restaurant spends hours sweating over the wine list to ensure that the guests have the right wines to pair with the just-introduced spring menu. The general manager walks the property daily to make sure guests and visitors are quasi-delirious. The caddies, even though they might have spent a few moments longer than necessary at a local gathering spot, arrive early and are willing to help you navigate the resort's courses and their many and varied hazards. And the golf professionals and the golf staff show up before dawn every day with the singular goal of making sure that all golfers have everything they need to enjoy their golf day. They can't swing the club for you on the first tee, but if they could, they would.

And then there's the golf, or to be more specific, the golf *courses*. Many of the finest courses in the world are private—so private that the chances of even a well-connected golfer getting on are slim to none at best. So the top golf destinations in the world provide anyone with the desire to play a top course with the opportunity. Yes, there's a price tag, but if you want to play Pinehurst No. 2, site of two very exciting U.S. Open Championships, it's right there. Ditto Pebble Beach. Ditto the highly regarded courses at Bandon Dunes. Want to play Augusta National? Highly unlikely unless your father-in-law is a member *and* he likes you. Want to play Pinehurst No. 2? Call 1-800-ITS-GOLF. When the person answers the phone, she will say, with passion, "It's a beautiful day in Pinehurst," even if it's bucketing down sleet and wintry mix outside. Within a week, or even less, you could be standing on the first tee of one of the top twenty golf courses on the planet.

The destinations in this chapter have not been chosen at random, but neither are the selections a "best of" list—empirical or otherwise. Nor have I listed them in any particular order. I chose them based on fame, enjoyment, reputation, and pilgrimage to reward quotient. I also considered (mightily) the quality of the golf. Some are resorts, while others are geographical areas. Either way, I firmly believe that every serious intelligent golfer should make the effort to visit one of these locations at least once. Some require somewhat arduous journeys (unless you have a private Bell Ranger or Citation X), and once you have arrived, all of them find ways to help you earn more credit card points than you thought possible in such a short period. But all of these must-plays represent resort and public-access golf at its very, very best.

You will not soon forget a visit to any of these locations. But perhaps most important, you will enjoy these spots because they are civilized without being overbearingly snobby. Each section includes a bit of insider information that should help you enjoy each destination a little bit more than the person who has not purchased this tome. I hope you enjoy these spots as much as I have enjoyed writing about them.

GREAT GOLF DESTINATIONS

PINEHURST RESORT
VILLAGE OF PINEHURST, NORTH CAROLINA
800.487.4653/910.295.6811
WWW.PINEHURST.COM

Pinehurst is one of the crown jewels of American golf. Opened in 1895 by James Walker Tufts, a Boston soda fountain entrepreneur and multimillionaire, the resort has provided golfers from around the world with more than a century of wonderful golf and relaxation in the idyllic, quiet, and bucolic sandhills of North Carolina. In the past decade, Pinehurst has augmented its already superb reputation through a series of improvements, additions, renovations, and events—most notably the hosting of the U.S. Open Championship in 1999 and 2005. To borrow some British phraseology, Pinehurst is currently in *excellent form.*

Located roughly between Charlotte and Raleigh in central North Carolina, Pinehurst sits on sandy soil, a geological abnormality in a state with a surfeit of sticky red clay. The *terroir* is thus perfect for golf: well-drained, gently undulating land dotted with tall pines. The scenery isn't jaw-dropping. The ocean is a three-hour drive, and there are no mountains to provide postcard backdrops for signature holes. Yes, there are adjunctive activities such as croquet, tennis, and lawn bowls, and you can book a chain of treatments at the spa, but the person who hates golf will likely be bored brainless staring at pine trees all day. Pinehurst is pure golf—powerful, undiluted, passionate, raw golf. For the intelligent golfer who wants golf and pretty much nothing else, it's paradise—a golfaholic's nirvana.

There always has been, and probably always will be, some mild confusion (and legal wrangling even) over the true meaning of the word *Pinehurst*. To some, primarily people who live in the Carolinas, it's the area in and around the resort, an area that includes more than thirty top-quality golf courses. To others, Pinehurst *is* the resort. For the sake of expediency, this section details just the resort, but I thoroughly encourage you to investigate the surrounding area—to travel off-campus, as it were.

The resort comprises the Carolina Hotel, the main clubhouse, and eight courses simply numbered one through eight—further proof of the purity of the golf. There's no "mountain course," "ocean view course," or "lake course" because there are no mountains, no nearby ocean, and no lakes of any real significance. Courses one through five are located around the main clubhouse while courses six, seven, and eight are separate entities. The hotel is about half a mile from the clubhouse, and there's a convenient shuttle if you don't want to walk. The overall operation is slick and well organized yet never demeaning or ostentatious. Immediately adjacent to the Carolina Hotel is the quaint Pinehurst Village with its boutiques, golf memorabilia stores, and eateries. Pinehurst is very much about stepping out of the daily routine and into a different place and world. Ditch the BlackBerry, the cell, and the laptop and unwind.

The resort boasts a pleasant variety of visitors, guests, and locals. Pinehurst is nowhere near a major airport, yet the resort attracts a busy conference and meeting business. The membership, mostly local golf-crazed retirees, is healthy, active, and omnipresent. Visiting groups of four to twenty, often the same people over and over, make a trip to the resort an annual event. Plus there are plenty of couples and foreign guests as well. The only common denominator is a love for the game and for the sweet pine scent that greets you as you approach the resort.

Those looking for chef-driven cuisine and big-time nightlife will want to go elsewhere. Pinehurst is not a party village, although it's possible on certain weekends to find some late-night activity. The food is wonderful, especially if you're a meat-and-potatoes guy or gal. You'll even find some southern delicacies at Pinehurst if you scour the menu.

Pinehurst has seasons. Summers can have volcanic heat, and there's always the possibility of a violent thunderstorm mid-to-late afternoon. Fall brings clear skies, less humidity, and pleasant temperatures, which means that October might be the best time for a visit. But Pinehurst was originally a winter resort, so while the weather is less predictable from December to mid-March, with a bit of luck you'll get fine conditions. Have you watched the Masters played every April? That describes the spring weather in Pinehurst, with flowering shrubs and trees included at no extra charge. The bottom line, weather-wise? Stay four days, and there's a better than 80 percent chance that you'll play golf every day.

But why not stay for eight days and take in all eight courses? Each has its own identity and vibe. The rock star is Pinehurst No. 2, site of the 1999 and 2005 U.S. Open Championship. It's a mysterious and fiendishly difficult golf course for an intelligent golfer of any standard, even though it looks relatively modest at first introduction. It's a fun course off the tee, with plenty of room, yet the approach shots are hugely difficult as the greens are relatively small but play even smaller. Jack Nicklaus famously said that landing a ball on a green at Pinehurst is like landing a ball on the top of a VW Beetle. Once your ball has rolled off the side of the turtle-backed greens, which it will, getting up and down requires the touch of a surgeon, the knowledge of a physics professor, and the guts of a paratrooper. Things can be going along fairly well at No. 2 for a few holes; then, *shazam*, there's an 8 on the scorecard—on a par-3.

The challenge with Pinehurst No. 2 is that it's an impossible course to get to know unless you play it about fifty times. There are keyholes, but they are hard to find—even with a caddy. There are answers to the questions that the course asks, but these too are never especially obvious. The course is a tough, tough examination. If you fail the first time, which you likely will, just remember that No. 2 got the better of the world's top golfers when they visited for the two U.S. Opens: there were lots of red faces and big numbers. Just ask John Daly what he thinks about the eighth hole. He had a double-digit score on the hole and even hit a ball while it was moving.

The good news at Pinehurst is that the other seven courses are more user-friendly and thus more enjoyable—at least for the intelligent golfer with a mid-handicap. Pinehurst No. 1 is a course that any club in the United States would be proud to own. It's nowhere near as difficult as No. 2, and the challenges are more obvious, but it's no pushover because it still features some of the dynamics that make No. 2 so totally impossible—like those humpbacked greens. For the first-time visitor to Pinehurst, No. 1 is a fine introduction. Pinehurst No. 3 looks short enough to be a ladies-only course, but it's well worth a visit and is fun—especially after the torture of No. 2. The tough, small greens require total concentration.

Architecturally, Pinehurst No. 4 has had a mixed background and complex history. That changed around 1998 when famous golf course architect Tom Fazio reengineered and redesigned the course to complement No. 2. In fact, several greens at No. 4 are more severe than the greens at No. 2, but thankfully, the course isn't as hard because the intelligent golfer can successfully approach each putting surface from different angles, making it significantly more enjoyable. Pinehurst No. 4 boasts a prettier piece of property, with some beautiful lakes and slightly more undulation. From the back tees, though, it's a worthy test for the scratch golfer. The defining feature of the course might be the brutal, deep pot bunkers that seem to be just about everywhere.

Relatively new by Pinehurst standards, Pinehurst No. 5 is the last course on the resort campus. The course has more elevation change and is slightly narrower in spots than the other courses; it's even quirky in places. The greens are not as severe, and the bunkering is not as punishing. The result is a hidden gem that's perhaps the most enjoyable of all the Pinehurst courses. It's a great first course to play as an introduction to the resort.

Pinehurst No. 6, No. 7, and No. 8 are just a short drive from the main resort; each course has its own character and own plot of land. Pinehurst No. 6 has had its fair share of tinkering over the years yet remains quintessential Pinehurst, with wide fairways and undulating greens. Generally hillier than the other Pinehurst courses, No. 6 has an excellent set of par-3s. George Fazio, Tom Fazio's uncle, designed the course in 1979, and Tom renovated it in 2005.

Pinehurst No. 7 is a curious course whose design and routing owe more to a phase in the life of Pinehurst when the then-ownership wanted to maximize real estate frontage and development. Architect Rees Jones said that when he got the commission to design No. 7, he stayed up all night working on the layout and, in places, it shows. There are too many holes with downhill drives and semi-blind uphill approach shots so that, after a while, the course develops a certain sameness. Just after 2000, Pinehurst hired Jones to renovate and redesign the course, and Jones removed the one characteristic that made No. 7 so interesting—a roughness around the edges. Still, No. 7 has its devotees who think it's one of the finest Pinehurst courses.

To celebrate its centennial, Pinehurst hired Tom Fazio to design Pinehurst No. 8, and that course might be the best course at the resort behind No. 2. Though a modern course in many ways, as soon as it opened in 1996, No. 8 looked like it had been there for decades. The land used to be the resort's shooting grounds, and it was a scrubby and rough piece of property dotted with wetlands—today's word for swamps. Fazio left much of the rough ground intact; thus, the course has a most un-Fazio-like rough-hewn look that augments the strategic interest and visual appeal. There's only one modest hole, the uphill par-4 third, but the others are really solid. A first-time visitor may find the greens a hair confusing, but they are not as hard as they look. Like today's well-designed modern courses, Pinehurst No. 8 is elastic: it has hosted a professional championship, yet *Golf for Women* magazine ranks it the sixteenth most woman-friendly golf course in the United States. While Pinehurst No. 2 is a must-play for its history and major championship appeal, No. 8 is the must-play for its ambiance and fun factor.

For a vivid sense of the history of the game, a couple of short walks at Pinehurst are mandatory—from the main entrance of the clubhouse to the golf shop, and the hallway of the Carolina Hotel that stretches from the administrative offices to the meeting rooms. In less than an hour, you'll discover the history not just of the resort, but also of American golf at the professional and amateur levels. Anyone who is anyone has won something at Pinehurst, and perhaps the finest U.S. Open took place at Pinehurst in 1999 when Payne Stewart won with a twelve-foot putt on the eighteenth hole. There's a large and wonderful bird's-eye photo of the scene in the hallway of the main clubhouse. Look closely at the photos, and you'll see famous professionals and mostly A-list celebrities. Study the boards that list past champions, and you'll come to know some of the most famous names in the game. On Sundays, Pinehurst No. 2 places all of the hole locations in the same spots as on the final day of the 1999 U.S. Open.

The most famous name at Pinehurst is Donald Ross, the Scottish-born professional golfer and golf course architect who made his winter home and developed his reputation at Pinehurst. He added holes to Pinehurst No. 1, then designed No. 2, No. 3, and No. 4. Guests who visited the resort from all over the United States subsequently asked Ross to design and build the courses in their communities. Ross visited only a fraction of the courses that bear his name, but his influence in early American golf cannot be understated—and it all began at Pinehurst. There's a statue of the great man just behind the eighteenth green of No. 2, and there's plenty of memorabilia in the clubhouse and main hotel. Make some time to soak it all up.

The other, totally essential way to get to know Pinehurst is with the assistance of one of the many fine caddies who work full time at Pinehurst. If you decide to play Pinehurst No. 2 or any of the other courses in a golf cart, go back to the hotel and work on your taxes instead—it's just not civilized. As Peggy Kirk Bell, owner of Pine Needles in nearby Southern Pines, says, "You haven't played golf until you've played a Donald Ross course with a caddy." The powers-that-be at

Pinehurst keep golf carts off the course at No. 2 anyway, so when you check in, make sure that you ask for a caddy. The professionals in the golf shop will send you downstairs to the unattractive basement where the caddy master will set you up. It's also fun, and wise, to hire a caddy when you play the other courses at Pinehurst, although you can carry your own bag on some of them. It seems a great shame to go to Pinehurst and drive around in a golf cart—it's rather like visiting the Museum of Modern Art in New York City while wearing a blindfold.

Once the sun begins to set, there's plenty of postround entertainment at Pinehurst, both at the resort and off. The main clubhouse has a restaurant and bar—fittingly called the 91st Hole. When the weather is pleasant, head outside to enjoy the libation while overlooking the massive practice putting green. The Holly Inn and the Manor Inn both have excellent restaurants; the main meal inside the main dining room at the Carolina is a formal affair, where men are required to wear a jacket. Courses No. 6, No. 7, and No. 8 also have bar areas. The only fourdiamond restaurant in the Pinehurst area is at the Holly Inn, which is part of the resort. The Holly also has what might be the best bar in the area—at least from an ambiance perspective. After dinner, repair to the Ryder Cup Lounge in the main clubhouse or go off-campus to the famous Pine Crest Inn. For an ever rowdier time, try Dugan's in the village—head straight downstairs to the tiny basement. Sometimes there's a band tucked into a corner. If you stay until closing and wake up the next morning feeling slightly piqued, visit Pinehurst's opulent spa.

Pinehurst isn't sexy and it's not a celebrity hangout or enclave, and that's part of its attraction. It's what golf was meant to be, perhaps . . . serene, charming, fun, inviting, and intelligent. As soon as you set foot on the property, you feel like part of the club and part of a history that dates to the very beginning of golf in the United States. And for that alone, it's well worth a visit.

Pebble Beach Resorts
Pebble Beach, California
800.654.9300
www.pebblebeach.com

Standing alone, without golf, Pebble Beach on California's Monterey Peninsula is the type of spot that sends the senses into total riot. It's one of the most magnificent and jaw-dropping locations in the United States, the climactic point perhaps of the rugged and wild West Coast. Thankfully for the intelligent golfer, there's a golf course there. Several, actually, the most famous of which is Pebble Beach Golf Links, which opened in 1919.

Eliciting glassy-eyed stares and moments of silence from even the most garrulous golfers, Pebble Beach is the resort that nobody wants to leave. The poster child for the ultimate in American golf luxury, location, and subtle decadence, it's the golf resort that nongolfers *really* want to visit. Pebble Beach dwarfs and renders inconsequential the various and sundry celebrities who pitch up for all those celebrity events the resort has hosted over the years. Pebble Beach is not exactly a secret—nor a hidden gem. Golfers from all over the world make the effort to get to Pebble Beach and enjoy all that the resort has to offer. For the lucky few, it's a regular indulgence. For most, it's a once-in-a-lifetime visit.

Located near Monterey and Carmel, about a two-hour drive south from San Francisco Airport, Pebble Beach sits directly on the Monterey Peninsula. Those who would rather avoid the drive from the Bay Area might want to consider using the Monterey Peninsula Regional Airport, which is a short drive from the golf and lodging.

Pebble Beach comprises four full-length golf courses: Pebble Beach Golf Links, the Links at Spanish Bay, Spyglass Hill Golf Course, and Del Monte Golf Course. There's also a short "Executive" nine-hole course called Peter Hay. You'll find a variety of resort-owned lodging as well: the Lodge at Pebble Beach, the Inn at Spanish Bay, and Casa Palmero.

There's also an expansive spa and several eateries. Anyone can play Pebble Beach, and anyone can stay at the resort, given the inclination. The resort offers a number of seasonal Stay and Play packages. The packages can be expensive, and sundry items like steaks and bottles of really good wine will inflate the final bill—a hair—but the value of visiting one of the finest golf courses anywhere makes the cost worthwhile.

Pebble Beach Golf Links (let's just call it Pebble Beach, shall we?) starts rather inconspicuously with three inland holes. Then the figure-eight routing dramatically brings the ocean into play at the fourth where a cliff borders the right side of the green. The first of Pebble Beach's truly epic holes is its shortest, the par-3 seventh, just 103 yards. The green seems to sit right in the middle of the Pacific, and the exposure makes club selection tricky. Anything from a lob wedge to a 4-iron might work. Someone someday probably had to hit driver. The par-4 eighth features perhaps the finest second shot in golf, an approach over a chasm to a tiny green; if this shot fails to get the blood pumping through the veins a little faster, then you have assumed room temperature. Anything to the right on the next two par-4s means trouble since the two holes are perched precariously next to the Pacific.

The start of the back nine heads inland through the Monterey Pines then emerges back to the cliffs at the end, most spectacularly at the seventeenth and the eighteenth, quite possibly the two foremost finishing holes in the game. The seventeenth features the famous hourglass green, where two-putting and getting up and down are extremely treacherous. The eighteenth is a glorious par-5. Sea otters frolic in the kelp below the tee, and from the tee, there's a decision to be made—play short of the tree on the right side of the fairway or take it on by bringing the sea to the left into play. Even after a successful tee shot, there's work ahead: Jack Nicklaus reached the green in two shots, but most resort golfers will need to lay up and hit an extremely precise wedge for the approach. Even if the round has not gone well to that point, a par at the last hole will make up for just about everything. Can you think of the vacation that was so good you never wanted to leave? That's the feeling you will likely have as you walk off the eighteenth at Pebble Beach.

Unless you play a lot of golf in the area or at a similar type of location, the grasses at Pebble Beach may seem unfamiliar; they certainly augment the difficulty. The mostly small greens at Pebble Beach feature *Poa annua*, a type of grass that can make for an extremely slick surface. It can also grow quickly, making for slightly bumpy surfaces late in the day, so an early tee time is always advisable. If you stray way off line, you might encounter a sticky substance that looks somewhat like grass but is actually ice plant; the only realistic option from this stuff is a wedge.

Even if Pebble Beach was located next to a nuclear waste dump, disused strip mine, or NASCAR track, intelligent golfers would play it for the quality of the routing and the strategic interest— the golf course is that good. But it's not located next to something awful. It's perched on a glorious piece of property. Pebble Beach is the golf course with everything: Looks. Brawn. Beauty. Charm. Brains. You name it. It's everything a golf course should be.

Just five miles from Pebble Beach is the beautiful offspring, the Links at Spanish Bay. Like Pebble Beach, Spanish Bay is set hard by the sea, but it's a different type of golf course, an "American" links, if you like, that looks and even plays like the real thing. It's a feat of modern golf course construction that Robert Trent Jones Jr., Tom Watson, and former U.S. Golf Association president Sandy Tatum designed and built. Even though the site is a former sand quarry, the builders and designers trucked in vast amounts of sand to create the genuine links effect. (Actually, it wasn't trucked in, it was brought in by conveyor belt.) After shaping the site, the design team sewed mostly fescue grasses—just like those on a typical British links.

Strategy and interest at Spanish Bay comes primarily from rippled and canted fairways, difficult stances, and really horrible pot bunkers just like the ones you might find at Muirfield or Royal Troon in Scotland. Spanish Bay is just a short drive from

Pebble Beach, and there's wind— often—and glorious views of the sea. But Spanish Bay provides the resort guest with a different type of golf that perfectly complements Pebble Beach.

There's more. A typical golf package at Pebble Beach includes a round at Spyglass Hill—which isn't exactly chopped liver. In 2003, *Golf Digest* ranked the course the fifth-best public course in the United States. So while you might be foaming at the mouth to get to the first tee at Pebble Beach or Spanish Bay, Spyglass Hill will be almost as rewarding. And no less difficult—three holes (the sixth, the eighth, and the sixteenth) are among the most difficult on the PGA Tour. If you're a Robert Louis Stevenson fan, you might recognize the name Spyglass Hill from the novel *Treasure Island*. When the course opened in 1966, the powers-that-be christened the holes using nomenclature from the novel. Robert Trent Jones Sr., one of the most influential American golf course architects, routed the first five holes through seaside dunes and the remaining holes through pine forest.

The fourth course at Pebble Beach is the Del Monte Golf Course, which holds the distinction of being the oldest continuously operating course west of the Mississippi. Del Monte is inland, just south of Monterey to the east of U.S. Highway 1. It's a fine golf course in its own right and has hosted significant events, including the California State Amateur Championship. The layout features narrow fairways and small-ish greens. If your Pebble Beach stay includes a round at Del Monte, don't panic. You will likely enjoy the day.

The golf at Pebble Beach is but half of the enjoyment equation. From the day the doors first opened at the resort in 1880, accommodations have been nothing less than sumptuous. Casa Palmero is a Spanish-style enclave located along the first and second fairways at Pebble Beach. With just twenty-four rooms and suites, it's perfect for the person or group who wants some privacy—although the "Main House" has a living room, library, heated pool, bar, and billiards room. The Inn at Spanish Bay is larger, with more than 250 rooms and suites, many with views of the Pacific. But if you think you might visit Pebble Beach only once and want to push the throttle through the floor, stay at the Lodge. A few days there will make you feel like you have moved to the Monterey Peninsula. Many of the rooms and suites have views of the eighteenth fairway and the Pacific, and most have working fireplaces. There's nothing cookie-cutter: the furniture for each room is individual, and you'll have more than enough space to unwind and relax. Why not go for a deluxe, one-bedroom suite that features a guaranteed view, a separate living room, and a whirlpool—among other goodies?

There are no fewer than seven eateries at the Lodge and six at the Inn at Spanish Bay. At the

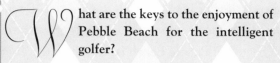

What are the keys to the enjoyment of Pebble Beach for the intelligent golfer?

ONE: Play the right set of tees. Go one forward of normal. Even at around 6,000 yards, most golfers will get all the golf they want, for example, at Spanish Bay.

TWO: Take advantage of the wonderful eateries at the resort.

THREE: Remember that *Poa annua* on the greens can be tricky stuff.

FOUR: Saddle up a caddy.

FIVE: Get your game in shape before you arrive. Two months before your visit to the Monterey Peninsula, make time for some lessons and plenty of practice. The views of the Pacific are inspirational—unless you are hacking and tearing up the hallowed turf. During your lessons, ask your teacher about strategies for playing in the wind.

SIX: Book well ahead—up to a year if you want the best rooms at peak times.

SEVEN: Buy and bring top-quality waterproof gear, including wet gloves (ask for them at your local golf shop).

EIGHT: Bring your spouse and make it a couple's gig. Lots of resorts say that they can accommodate nongolfers. Pebble Beach is one of the few that can back it up.

Lodge, Club XIX, open for dinner only, offers the most serious dining with its contemporary American menu. If fowl is your game, try the Maple Leaf Duck Breast roasted in the oven with Sautéed Cherries and Potato Gratin with Leg Confit Orange-Vanilla Jus. The restaurant offers a strong wine list as well. For something more casual, the Tap Room is a long-time favorite—a steak house but also a pub, with several beers on tap and in the bottle. Or try a Del Monte Fizz, a delightful chemistry experiment fusing orange and lemon juice, gin, cream, egg white, vanilla extract, and sugar. At the Inn at Spanish Bay, those looking for a clubby or sports bar feel might visit either Sticks or Traps; Traps has a late-night menu. The most serious restaurant is Peppoli, which features a Tuscan menu, top Italian wines, and long views over the golf course and the ocean.

There's really no significant need to leave the resort, but if you must, you'll find some famous restaurants nearby. For fresh fish, try Passion Fish in Monterey; the wine list has a superb selection of local wines. In Carmel, go to Casanova, an intimate and romantic spot with a menu that's a step beyond eclectic. The lady who owned the building before it became a restaurant apparently used to cook for Charlie Chaplin. The wine cellar has around 30,000 bottles, and the maître d' will give you a tour if you ask politely.

The marketing people at Pebble Beach like to use the words "links" and "Scotland" and "Scottish," and there's often a bagpiper piping away near the main campus or the Inn at Spanish Bay. The weather on the Monterey Peninsula can be just as fickle as in Scotland. The coast often creates its own weather, and while it can be clear as a bell and warm at Spanish Bay, it might be fogged in and damp at Pebble Beach. On your anointed day to play the great course, it could be raining sideways or be almost summer-like—in February. Or July. But it's highly unlikely that you'll get any snow; the white stuff falls about once every forty years.

There's a lot of history at Pebble Beach. The AT&T National Pro-Am is the successor to the Bing Crosby-led "Clam Bake" that started in 1947. There have been some huge moments, such as Tom Watson's miraculous victory over Jack Nicklaus at the 1982 U.S. Open. Or Tom Kite's one and only major championship ten years later. And then, in 2000, Tiger Woods brought the course to its knees and won the U.S. Open by a staggering fifteen shots. But even without those important pieces of golf history, Pebble Beach would be just fine. It's not really about history at Pebble Beach; it's about the setting and the fact that there's golf—great golf, perhaps the greatest in America—right in the middle of one of America's most gloriously beautiful locations.

BANDON DUNES GOLF RESORT
BANDON, OREGON
888.345.6008
WWW.BANDONDUNESGOLF.COM

In 1999, something totally remarkable took place on the remote southern coast of Oregon. A man with a dream, Mike Keiser, opened a golf course called Bandon Dunes. The course was designed by a mostly unknown young Scottish architect, David McLay Kidd, on what initially looked like unusable gorse-scrub but turned out to be genuine linksland—the type of coastal, sandy, dunes-like property rare even in Scotland. After torturous years of clearing, bureaucracy, and sheer grunt work, Keiser and Kidd gave birth to the real thing: a genuine links course. But it wasn't in the British Isles, it was in America. It was a risk, specifically the type of "if we build it, will they come?" type of risk, for Bandon is (with apologies to all Bandonians) pretty much slap-bang in the middle of nowhere. There isn't a major city within easy driving distance. The nearest regional airport, thirty minutes away, offers minimal service. For all intents and purposes, it's a day to get there and a day to get back, even if you have a personal jet at your beck and call. You can get to Portland, which is not that hard, but it's at least four hours by car from there. Eugene? Almost three hours. At the beginning, Keiser had to wonder if anyone would come—especially in today's fast-paced world.

They came.

Initially, they came because every golf course architecture writer in every golf magazine got almost teary about the place after his or her initial reconnaissance trip. The first paying visitors got gushy after making the journey; thus by word-of-mouth and through the written word, the word got out that Bandon was something amazingly special and that the trek was worth it. There are three courses now (by Kidd, Tom Doak, and the team of Bill Coore and Ben Crenshaw) and more visitors and even more accolades, but Bandon Dunes has retained its low-key charm. It's walking only, usually with a caddy. There's excellent dining now but still without much fanfare. The accommodations are pleasant enough, but it's not the palatial stuff of upscale travel magazines. At Bandon Dunes, it's *all* about the golf. Everything else is pretty much an afterthought or adjunct.

To understand Bandon Dunes fully, it's important to know something about David McLay Kidd and his background. Kidd was the son of a greenkeeper (nowadays called a golf course superintendent). As a child, Kidd spent his summers on the west coast of Scotland at Machrihanish, home of the Machrihanish Golf Club, which has a highly acclaimed links course right next to the Atlantic Ocean. Kidd remains a member of the club, and while Bandon Dunes isn't "Machrihanish America," the influence is clear. If there's no wind, you can get around mostly in the air, but if it's windy or slightly inclement, then the ground game is the viable and preferred option. Speaking of options, there are plenty of them from tee to green— just as there are at Machrihanish. And just like its cousin in Scotland, Bandon Dunes has character and charm yet can be moody and capricious.

Off the tee, Bandon Dunes is mostly open. But the best route to attacking most of the holes requires more accuracy than sheer power. The other key to success at Bandon Dunes is avoiding the thoroughly horrible and nasty bunkers. The finest hole? It might be the par-4 sixteenth that, with some help from the prevailing summer wind, might be drivable, even at 366 yards. It's right by the beach, with some of the course's best views of the Pacific—and that's saying something; it's a hole with some brains to accompany the beauty, because taking on the green with the driver is not without some risk.

Kidd likens the course to a symphony with what he describes as "a strong start, a sense of anticipation, small crescendos, and an incredible finishing sequence along the Pacific." Most of the top architects in the world must have been begging Mike Keiser for the chance to compose Bandon's first symphony. His risk with Kidd paid off handsomely, and both Kidd and Bandon Dunes have moved on to greater work. Recently, Kidd got another plum assignment, the newest course at St. Andrews.

Tom Doak designed the next course at Bandon Dunes, which is named Pacific Dunes. If you ever meet a big name (or even a little name) golf course architect, have some fun and mention Tom Doak. It will be amusing for you but will create severe pain for the architect. Doak is the *enfant terrible* of the industry, primarily because he dared to criticize the work of his fellow architects in his must-read, must-have book, *The Confidential Guide to Golf Courses*. The book is out of print, and copies fetch close to $300 on eBay. Why? Because it's brutally honest and is one of the few golf course guides that tells it like it is. Doak has further annoyed the top golf course architects by becoming hugely successful and by being able to do it his way. Exhibit No. 1 is Pacific Dunes, a course that's every bit the equal of Bandon Dunes and might even be a bit better. Doak and his team have produced a strong portfolio of top courses around the world, yet Pacific Dunes might be his finest work to date. It's easily a candidate for best new course of the last forty years—and that's saying something. Much of the success of the course again comes from the site or, to use golf architect lingo, the canvas.

On that canvas, Doak painted eighteen excellent holes. One of the keys to the success of the course is the consistency—one fantastic hole after another.

The fourth is a cliff-top hole that any course would love to own, but it's not the best hole on the course even though it's tremendously scenic. Candidates for the top spot include the tenth and eleventh, both right by the ocean. The seventeenth, a 210-yard par-3 with a bank of deep gorse behind the hole, might seem intimidating, but there's a relatively easy way to play the hole for the golfer without the game to take on the left-hand hole locations: just play to the right side of the massive green and let the ball funnel down. The climactic hole is a monster par-5 at almost 600 yards (591, to be exact). To this point, the course has not been silly long, but given the wrong wind direction, this hole might lead to a big number.

By design, Pacific Dunes looks rough around the edges, which might make it look harder than it actually plays. The great thing about Pacific Dunes is that it's fun to play, even for the mid- to high-handicapper. From the next-to-last tees, the course is around 6,100 yards, and even from the very back tees, it's a modest 6,633 yards—not a backbreaker by any stretch of the imagination. Plus there are keyholes and shortcuts that you can try to discover for yourself or, better still, let a caddy help you find. A round at Pacific Dunes could be slightly tortuous if you find some of the more unforgiving bunkers (one of them is eighteen feet deep!), but with some sound navigation, Pacific Dunes should be a lot of fun.

For the third course at Bandon Dunes, called Bandon Trails, Keiser hired the golf course architecture team of Ben Crenshaw and Bill Coore, creators of some of the most impressive modern courses in the past fifteen years. Modern might be the wrong word, though. Coore and Crenshaw are part of the "throwback" movement in golf course architecture. The goal has been to incorporate the best aesthetic and strategic elements of early golf course architects such as Donald Ross, H.S. Colt, and Alister MacKenzie. Following Bandon Dunes and Pacific Dunes was always going to be a challenge, so Coore and Crenshaw took a slightly different tack, moving inland and creating what would be a pleasant hike if you did not have your golf bag with you. The course happily boasts a sensational variety of terrain that few, if any courses, can claim; it might even seem a touch schizophrenic. Bill Coore provides some insight in the first pages of the yardage book:

> *As its name implies, Bandon Trails will take you on a walk, if you will, through windswept dunes, meadows of vegetation framed by indigenous shrubbery, and through woodlands of towering fir and spruce trees. Sometimes the journey and the golf will be wild and tumultuous, sometimes serene.*

The course seamlessly integrates the finest architectural features of the finest golf course architects. It uses the natural terrain superbly to produce yet another course at Bandon Dunes that all but the most hackneyed and myopic golfer should thoroughly enjoy; certainly, the intelligent golfer will. At times, you'll feel like you're at Pinehurst. At others, you'll feel like you are west of London at one of the heathland courses. On some holes, the feeling is very much like the Australian sand belt courses. So the trail that is the theme at Bandon Trails feels almost like a world golf tour in eighteen holes. And that's a good thing: golf at Bandon Trails is the antithesis of U.S. Open golf, where the course and its setup tell where you must go. At Bandon Dunes, each hole on each course offers options galore, and this alone makes the golf a lot more fun.

The resort brochure describes a surprising range of things for the nongolfer to enjoy, but the person who absolutely abhors golf might find very little of interest—aside from whale or bird watching. However, the river fishing is supposed to be excellent.

When it's finally dark and you have returned from what has likely been thirty-six holes, there's plenty of sustenance at one of five spots. The most upscale, even though you won't need to dress up, is the Gallery Restaurant, a chef-driven location quietly building an impressive wine list to complement its seafood and aged beef. McKee's Pub offers a traditional bar menu, along with a wide selection of microbrews, most from the Northwest, plus single malt scotches; there's a small and sheltered dining room upstairs. The Tufted Puffin Lounge is a quiet place for a drink with friends or a drink before dinner at the Gallery. Later at night, you may find yourself at the manly enclave known as the Bunker Bar. And those who are playing Bandon Trails will want to stop in Trails End, which overlooks the eighteenth green.

Accommodations at Bandon Dunes are far from spartan but aren't stratospherically luxurious. As with the general dining setup, everything is geared toward the male golfer: many of the rooms feature large-screen high-definition televisions, which, as any man will tell you, is much, much more important than feather pillows and lavender hand cream. The Grove Cottages are specifically designed for a foursome; there's a gathering room with a fireplace and four separate bedrooms, each with a king bed and private bath. The Lodge has more variety, anything from single rooms to four-bedroom suites. The powers-that-be determined the golf courses would get the best land, so anyone looking for a beautiful sea view from the Lodge will be disappointed—for all the right reasons.

The intelligent golfer visiting Bandon Dunes can expect just about anything at any time weather-wise, but there's typically less rain from May through October. The area can receive significant rainfall, around seven inches a month in the winter, although locals believe there's a window of decent weather in February. The rates at Bandon Dunes clearly reflect the seasonal delineations. For best results, head out there when the chances for a wash-out are minimal.

For such a nascent resort, Bandon Dunes has earned some remarkable accolades and rankings from the golf media. In *Golf Magazine*, all three courses are currently ranked in the top 100 in the world; Pacific Dunes is ranked No. 13. In the same publication, Pacific Dunes ranked ahead of Pebble Beach in the "Top 100 You Can Play" list, and all three Bandon Dunes courses are in that list's top ten. Among the golf course architecture cognoscenti, things are moving along pretty well at Bandon Dunes. And Tom Doak designed Old MacDonald, the newest course.

The quality of the design at Bandon Dunes is clearly strong, but there's more to the success of the resort than solid landscape architecture. What has made Bandon Dunes such a success? The answer lies in the dirt. The soil and the terrain provide the visitor with real links golf—and real links golf is *golf in color*; everything else is monochromatic. Links golf, as opposed to routine parkland golf, has its quirks, its challenges, and its uncertainties, something the intelligent golfer understands and accepts, but the intelligent golfer also understands and appreciates that true links golf awakens the golf imagination, electrifies the golf senses, and produces a completely new golfer who suddenly starts to think about the many different ways to get the ball from the tee to the hole.

Should I hit it low here? Should I try to bounce it into the green? Can I take on that bunker over there? Should I putt or chip or hit a flop? I think I'll see if I can slingshot the ball off that mound toward the hole location today. What's the wind doing? The yardage says 154, but I think I'll punch a 5-iron. I'm going to ignore the yardage book; my eyes tell me it's a 135-yard shot. I'll go with that.

At Bandon Dunes, you'll find all the key ingredients to true links golf, including plenty of ball-eating gorse, fast and firm playing conditions, and little or no separation between the fairway and the green. Links golf is forty times more enjoyable than "other" golf, and while a million courses call themselves "a links course," pretty much the only true way to get the pedal-to-the-metal links effect in the United States is at Bandon Dunes. For that reason alone, it's the place every intelligent golfer should strive to visit. Remember: even on the most overcast day, links golf is *golf in color.*

The American Club
Kohler, Wisconsin
800.344.2838
www.destinationkohler.com

Perhaps the American Club in Kohler, Wisconsin, should be called the Hotel of the American Dream. In 1873, in the middle of an economic recession, John Michael Kohler, a young Austrian who had just moved to the United States, purchased a foundry and started to manufacture farm implements and other items. Ten years later, Kohler invented a new type of bathroom and launched the plumbing side of the business. The rest is history, success, and the stuff of American business legend.

In 1918, the Kohler Company built an attractive dormitory to house immigrant workers. Today, the same building is on the *National Register of Historic Places* and is now the American Club; just in case there's some confusion as to the country we're in, there's a 100-foot-tall flagpole outside the club—complete with a massive American flag. With its Tudor architectural style and slate roof, it's a stately building that houses guests from around the world who visit Kohler for a variety of reasons, but often just for the excellent Pete Dye golf. Kohler is a big-time celebration of American business acumen, ingenuity, passion, and drive. It's a destination that intelligent golfers, as well as nongolfers, can and should enjoy. Most of all, in a wonderfully friendly Midwestern way, Kohler might be the most civilized destination golf resort in the upper-tier states.

There are two places to stay, the American Club (which includes the Carriage House) and the Inn on Woodlake. Kohler has four first-rate golf courses, two at Blackwolf Run and two at Whistling Straits, on the western shore of Lake Michigan. As befits a company that produces some of the world's finest bathroom fixtures and accessories, the spa is beyond opulent. To complete the package, the dining options offer some of the finest meals in the Midwest—which is saying something when you consider that cities like Chicago, St. Louis, Cincinnati, and Milwaukee are home to some of the most wonderful eateries in the world. The American Club is the only AAA Five-Diamond resort hotel in the Midwest.

The resort is part of the charming village of Kohler, home to about 2,000 residents and headquarters of the Kohler Company. The concierge at the American Club can organize tours of the village. The success of the company and the development of Kohler as a resort destination is the work of Kohler chairman, president, and CEO, Herbert V. Kohler, a serious golfer who has put his personal passion into everything—and it shows.

The American Club is not only an opulent place to stay but is also a way for Kohler to display its finest furniture and bath fittings—all top-of-the-line and state-of-the-art—part of the "Gracious Living" credo that drives much of what happens at Kohler. The Carriage House, part of the American Club compound, houses the spa. And it's the type of spa that even someone who usually avoids spas should try—because it's Kohler and it's where the company gets to strut its stuff. If you want to bring spa-type opulence into your own room, go for one of the Immersion Suites, which includes a Kohler whirlpool bath. The "other" place to stay at Kohler is the Inn at Woodlake, which boasts a more modern look but is just as comfy as the American Club.

Kohler clearly takes its dining seriously—perhaps more so than at other top resorts. There are eleven eateries and restaurants. The flagship among them is the Immigrant Restaurant in the main body of the American Club. The Immigrant serves contemporary cuisine featuring plenty of local fare, and the layout revolves around a series of six rooms with French, Dutch, German, Norman, Danish, and English motifs reflecting the ethnicities of early Wisconsin settlers. There's a big wine list to complement the serious dining. But plenty at Kohler is less formal, and the pick of these might be the Horse and Plow, a pub that occupies the former site of the tap room when the American Club was the immigrant dormitory. The menu is pub fare (try the Chicken Pot Pie), and the expansive beer menu features some of the world's best.

Of course, what really matters is the golf, and the golf is so good that Kohler, despite its relative youth, has hosted several major championships, including the U.S. Women's Open and the PGA Championship.

Pete Dye designed all the courses at Kohler. As previously mentioned, there are two golf campuses at Kohler: Blackwolf Run and Whistling Straits. Let's start at the latter because that's the newer spot, and it's home to the course that most recently hosted a big event, specifically the 2004 PGA Championship. There are two courses at Whistling Straits: the Straits Course and the Irish. At Bandon Dunes, the land was there for pure links golf. At Whistling Straits, there was land along a major body of water but no genuine linksland. No problem. Dye simply created linksland using healthy doses of sand, fescue, and imagination. Not to mention time—and investment. The result is something truly special. Ditto the Irish Course that is less Irish than the Straits course but no less pleasing to the eye and another great walk. It's inland from the lake yet still has a links look. The main hazards are the four streams that crisscross the routing.

Dye is the golf course architect that every golf course architect wants to be, just like every film director and producer always wanted to be Stanley Kubrick, the guy who could do whatever he wanted and still keep the studios mostly happy. Nobody designs golf courses like Pete Dye, and nobody ever will. Dye's most famous course, which features an island seventeenth green, is at TPC Sawgrass. Because that course is there to defeat—and that's the right word—the best professional golfers, Dye has a reputation for building golf courses that are too hard for mere mortals.

But Dye builds reliable golf courses that are entertaining and fun—for everyone. There are bunkers perched on top of mounds and ravines and bunkers fronted by stacked telegraph poles or railroad ties. The general advice to any resort guest applies here; if it's your first time playing golf at Kohler, play a tee up from your normal tee. You'll enjoy yourself much more, especially when you come to a green complex that only Pete Dye could have dreamt up, the eighteenth at the Straits Course that is literally shaped like an irregular cross. The name of the hole? Dyeabolical. Thanks, Pete!

The first two courses at Kohler are also Dye creations, but they couldn't be more different from the Whistling Straits courses. Named for an Indian chief, Blackwolf Run is what the British call "parkland" golf—a catch-all term for pretty much any course that's not on linksland next to the sea. Blackwolf Run offers two courses, the River Course and the Meadow Valleys Course. River is the star, running adjacent to the Sheboygan River for most of its routing, often with interesting effect. For example, the ninth hole essentially offers the intelligent golfer three fairways from which to choose. It's a gambler's hole and a gambler's course: pull off the shot and you're sitting pretty; fail and you're not. Who knew that this bucolic a setting could produce golf this exciting?

Meadow Valleys offers a wider variety of terrain, and instead of the river, lakes provide the water hazards. It's not as hard as the River Course, but it's just as interesting and just as much fun. The hole that's most likely to get the heart of the intelligent golfer racing is the par-3 fifteenth, 227 yards from the back tees and 196 from the regular tees. It's a "hit me or else" hole with no bailout; thankfully, there's a huge green.

Kohler clearly operates on a national scale and caters to an international clientele. It's certainly a must-visit for Midwesterners. The American Club is about two hours from Chicago and about one hour from Milwaukee or Green Bay. It's also one of the most nongolfer-friendly resorts anywhere, with its opulent spa, the village, and most important, the Kohler Design Center. The Center will get anyone who is thinking about a touch of remodeling very much in the mood for a total home makeover. But most of all, Kohler provides the perfect example of what happens when American pride, American enterprise, American service, American creativity, and American golf collide.

St. Andrews Links Trust
St. Andrews. Fife, Scotland
+44.0.1334.466666
WWW.STANDREWS.ORG.UK

St. Andrews is not a resort in the traditional American sense. It's a living, breathing town with a university and a life of its own beyond the golf, a town with an ancient and sometimes tragic history. It's also the home of golf and the site of the world's first true links, subtly christened the Old Course. Unlike any other course in the world, the Old Course has no architect and no clear opening date, yet it remains one of the world's finest golf courses and a worthy test for the intelligent golfer under any conditions.

Nobody really knows whether the Old Course was the *first* golf course. But it's certainly the oldest in continuous operation. Something was probably going on as early as 1457, when the Scottish Parliament banned golf. It's tough to keep people away from their addiction to the game, though both James III (in 1471) and James IV (in 1491) repeated the ban. But James IV saw the light and the error of his previous legislation a few years later in 1502 and bought his first set of golf clubs. In 1552, through the work of Archbishop John Hamilton, a charter confirmed the rights of people who lived in St. Andrews to play golf on the links. Golf continued merrily in what must have been an informal fashion until a group formed the Society of St. Andrews Golfers, the predecessor of the current Royal and Ancient Golf Club.

The original Old Course had twenty-two holes (some say twenty-three), but the new society whittled that down to eighteen—and that's the reason every full course in the world has eighteen holes. The Society of St. Andrews Golfers established the initial rudimentary rules of golf, and outside the United States and Mexico, the Royal and Ancient (R&A) is the official rules body. The R&A's stone clubhouse sits just behind the first tee of the Old Course, and the R&A organizes numerous championships in the United Kingdom, including the Open Championship, often called the British Open.

Because golf is a massive part of the fabric of the town, St. Andrews is every intelligent golfer's second home. It's one of the most welcoming golf locations anywhere, and while it hosts hundreds of thousands of visitors every year, St. Andrews has avoided becoming too touristy—a remarkable achievement. The official St. Andrews golf portfolio comprises seven courses, including the most recent addition, the Castle Course. David McLay Kidd, who also designed the first course at Bandon Dunes, built St. Andrews' latest addition.

The Old Course sits on public land. On Sundays, as befits strict Presbyterian traditions, the course is closed unless it's hosting a championship. Instead of golfers marching through the course, you'll see "normal" people walking their dogs and simply enjoying a pleasant stroll on and around the links. Because no private entity owns the Old Course or the other courses that are part of the St. Andrews portfolio, they are technically open to everyone. The Old Course, in addition to being the mother and father of all golf courses, is, essentially, a municipal operation. But if you think you can just roll up to the course and walk on, as you might at a typical "muny," think again. A guaranteed tee time on the Old Course in the summer is gold dust, although, ironically, some golfers roll up and walk on having entered the daily ballot.

The governing entity at St. Andrews is the St. Andrews Links Trust, which comprises two committees—policy and management. In the past fifteen years or so, perhaps bowing to the pressure of supply and demand (mostly the latter), the Links Trust has organized golf at St. Andrews into more of a resort, with packages, more courses, and a more commercial approach. The moves have been controversial, especially among locals and golf tour operators, both hungry for guaranteed tee times. But when every golfer in the world wants to play at the home of golf and there are only so many tee times, a touch of commercial organization is inevitable—and wise. Once you understand the ins and outs, it can also work in your favor.

Even if golf history is not the part of the game that you find most fascinating, it's useful to understand a bit about the history of this great place. One gentleman you should get to know is Old Tom Morris (1821–1908), who was born in St. Andrews and was one of the instrumental figures in the development of the modern game. Allan Robertson, the first professional golfer, actually hired Morris. Both of these most intelligent golfers lie buried at St. Andrews.

As the professional, Morris was a renaissance man, in charge of everything from making clubs to mowing the greens. Old Tom designed many superb Scottish courses and was an excellent player, winning the Open Championship several times. He still holds the record as the oldest winner, at age forty-six. Morris's son, Young Tom Morris, was also a champion but died tragically in his twenties. Prestwick, Carnoustie, Muirfield, and Machrihanish are just a few of the courses that owe their success to Old Tom. When you visit St. Andrews, stop by the British Golf Museum just a short walk from the R&A clubhouse. It's a place that every intelligent golfer should tour, museum fan or not.

A word first about the "other" courses at St. Andrews. The New Course was the second course at St. Andrews and opened next to the Old Course in April 1895. Designed in part by Old Tom Morris, it's as pure a links course as can be found in Scotland; if it weren't immediately adjacent to the most famous golf course in the world and was its own entity with its own club, it would be more highly regarded. The New Course has gorse, a shared green, pot bunkers, and fine, tight turf perfect for running golf. The Jubilee Course is strong enough to hold qualifying events for major championships, but when it opened in 1897, it was originally meant to be a course for juniors and ladies. It's called Jubilee because it celebrates the Diamond Jubilee (sixty years) of the reign of Queen Victoria. In subsequent years, the powers-that-be have extended and modernized the course so that it's a solid test for any intelligent golfer. The Eden Course is the work of the most unsung of golf course architects, Harry Shapland Colt. It's less demanding, and thus more fun, than the first three courses at St. Andrews but still has a natural and uncontrived feel.

It would be almost eighty years before a new major course opened at St. Andrews. Named the Strathyrum Course, it is shorter than its sister courses at St. Andrews and has only fifteen bunkers, all of which are cunningly placed. It might seem easier on paper but still requires significant skill to score well. The Balgove Course is the type of course that every community needs: a 1,520-yard, nine-hole course primarily for junior golfers and beginners—a nursery course, if you will. If you have only a few days in town, then you will likely play other courses, but if you have time, then go out and have some fun. The seventh at St. Andrews is the Castle Course. Located on the other side of St. Andrews from the Old Course, the Castle is located on former farmland on some shallow cliffs, providing excellent views and some elevation changes.

Now to the star attraction, the one that everyone wants to see, meet, and get to know, the Old Course at St. Andrews. The first and eighteenth holes are located right in the town, which is superbly cool, but aside from that, the Old Course may seem slightly underwhelming. The views across the estuary are fine but not jaw-dropping, and the land, at first glance, looks Florida flat. The first hole, with its driving range-wide fairway, seems like a total yawner at just 370 yards from the back tees. Yet once the round begins, it becomes clear there's much more to St. Andrews than meets the eye. There was no golf course architect to move a lot of dirt and try to create something visually appealing. A few architects have tinkered here and there, but the course remains mostly unchanged. For this reason, the Old Course boasts a number of features that few, if any, golf course architects would consider, including a number of large double greens, some of which slope away from the fairway. Sometimes the Old Course might seem unfair: a mound in front of the fourth green will send a straight shot almost sideways; the twelfth has a cluster of nasty bunkers in the middle of the fairway right where a well-struck drive would land; and Jack Nicklaus has repeatedly said that he's not really sure how to play the approach shot to the seventeenth, the famous Road Hole, where the challenge is to thread the shot between a dismal pot bunker and a narrow road to a shallow green that's set about ninety degrees to the fairway. At a municipal course, the golfers would likely view the hole as a total abomination. At St. Andrews, it's brilliant—and rightfully so.

The Road Hole is the most heralded at St. Andrews, with its semi-blind tee shot perilously close to the Old Course Hotel, followed by the exacting approach. But the Old Course is much more than the seventeenth: its hole-to-hole consistency keeps it among the world's best courses. It helps if the wind is blowing, but even without a fresh breeze, a professional will have to think his way around. The first, with a burn (creek) in front of the green, demands instant respect. The muscular fifth is a well-earned par. The fourteenth, the longest par-5, is brilliant, and the final hole, even though it's short for a closing hole, always provides drama and the opportunity for a closing birdie. There are names for the key features on the course: Hell Bunker, the Principal's Nose, the Spectacles. Due to the long, thin, out-and-back routing, many of the bunkers come into play on more than one hole.

Enjoying St. Andrews the first time requires skill and patience, especially when the weather is poor and the wind is up. But most of all, St. Andrews requires a game plan. And the best way to plan is with the help of a St. Andrews caddy—who can, at the very least, tell you where to aim. Follow his (or her) advice, and you'll enjoy the first time at St. Andrews so much that you'll want to come back every year.

For many intelligent golfers, a golf trip to Scotland would not be worth the time or money without a round on the Old Course at St. Andrews. And with good reason. Thus a dead certain tee time is vital. There are two ways to get a tee time, but only one is guaranteed. The first is the daily ballot, a lottery, and it is not guaranteed until St. Andrews lets you know the day before your tee time. About 50 percent of all starting times are ballot-based. Your chances of success vary depending on the weather, the time of the year, and the sheer volume of golfers milling around St. Andrews hoping to play the Old Course. The results are available on the St. Andrews Links Trust Web site at around four in the afternoon. The lottery is just that, and thousands of golfers leave St. Andrews every month without the chance to play the world's first golf course.

Planning ahead for the guaranteed tee time means planning as much as two years in advance, especially if you choose to organize the trip by yourself. By mid-2007, all the available public bookable tee times for 2008 had been snapped up. So without going through the Old Course Experience or a golf tour operator who has not used his or her allotment, the only way to guarantee a tee time would be to book at least a year and a half ahead when those tee times become available. That's just the way it is.

There is a third option: the Old Course Experience, a program organized by the St. Andrews Links Trust with local hotels and tour operators. Essentially, you purchase a package based around a guaranteed tee time on the Old Course. Everything flows from that day and that time. Packages—and you have to go with a package—include green fees, luxury accommodations, and other sundry items including tee times on other St. Andrews courses. The Old Course Experience is an excellent option if you:

✦ Book late.

✦ Only want to hang around St. Andrews.

✦ Don't have a golf tour operator.

✦ Absolutely have to play the Old Course.

✦ Enjoy luxury-style places to stay.

✦ Have a relatively small group with some degree of flexibility.

If you are going to Scotland to play the Old Course and you rightfully feel that you want to play other famous Scottish courses (and maybe some Irish ones, too), then the best bet is to find a reputable and

*H*ere's some general advice about going to Scotland:

✦ Groups of four to eight work best, but larger groups can do well.

✦ If you want to play the Old Course at St. Andrews, make sure that your tour specialist has a guaranteed tee time for you. Don't leave home without it!

✦ Buy the best waterproof gear you can find.

✦ Get your game in shape, and take some lessons to work on some of the shots you'll need.

✦ Whenever possible, take a caddy. Your tour operator can guarantee caddies.

✦ Self-driving is okay, but having a bus and a bus driver makes all the difference.

✦ Take a jacket and tie.

✦ Many of the places where you will play are private clubs; behave accordingly.

✦ Get organized at least eighteen months ahead of your trip.

✦ If you are after the ultimate trip and are tight on time, think about getting from A to B in a helicopter.

✦ Luxury hotels are not often that luxurious in Scotland— by American standards.

✦ If your spouse is coming and hates golf, there's plenty to do, but make sure your group is well organized. Plan ahead for the nongolfers as you would for the golfers.

+ Try Haggis at least once. Ditto Black Pudding.

+ The less you rush and try to squeeze in as many courses as possible, the more you will enjoy the trip. It's difficult to see everything in Scotland in a week and still enjoy the golf. Ditto Ireland.

+ Seek out some hidden gems and off-the-beaten-path courses and clubs. Visits to the less-famous and somewhat mysterious courses are often more rewarding than the big-name clubs. Your chances of mingling with the locals improve, and that can lead to a lot of fun.

+ Listen to your specialist! They know the lay of the land and the places that your group will enjoy.

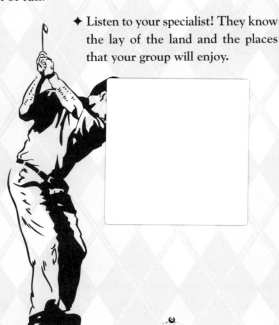

experienced golf tour specialist either in Scotland or the United States. There are plenty of reliable operators, and the best way to start is to ask the head golf professional at your course. He or she will probably know at least one specialist who can meet your needs. Many club professionals put together their own trips with members, and this can often be the best way to go because the pro acts as a guide and organizes games and related activities among the group.

In St. Andrews, there are some wonderful places to stay. And there's a good range of options, as well. The most famous is the Old Course Hotel right next to the Road Hole, the epic seventeenth. In fact, the hotel is so close that it's part of the hole's strategy: the best tee shot travels over a corner of the property. It's a Kohler resort now, part of the Kohler Company that also runs the American Club and its four courses. The Old Course Hotel was never downscale, but it's even more upscale now that Kohler has taken the reins. Another famous St. Andrews hotel is Rusacks, next to the eighteenth fairway of the Old Course. If you're a right-hander with a bad slice, you might be visiting it more often than you would like. There are some wonderful country house and estate-style hotels just outside St. Andrews, and these typically offer more space and pampering than hotels in town.

St. Andrews lies in the Kingdom of Fife, which is a somewhat hyperbolic way of saying that it's in

Fife County or the County of Fife. Close to forty non-St. Andrews courses reside in the Kingdom, and many of these are well worth a visit. Crail Golfing Society has two fine links courses. The Duke's Course near St. Andrews is now part of the Kohler ownership of the Old Course Hotel; the Duke's is a heathland course not unlike the ones west of London. Kingsbarns is a modern classic just minutes from the Old Course; it has wonderful views of the sea and is a tough test. And Lundin Golf Club is another hidden gem that too many people miss in their mania to play as much golf as possible in St. Andrews itself. A party of touring golfers could quite easily stay in St. Andrews for two weeks and enjoy a ton of wonderful golf without playing the same course twice. In fact, the first-time visitor to Scotland is well advised to stay put in St. Andrews and simply explore the town and the environs.

A visit to Scotland would not be complete without at least one round with a caddy (often spelled *caddie* in the United Kingdom). There are few callings, professions, or vocations that mix well with adult refreshment. You cannot be a race car driver or a pilot if you like to drink a lot—not just occasionally, but every day. But in Scotland, you can be a caddy and also someone who spends a significant amount of time in the pub. Early in the morning, you may find that the vapors coming from your caddy have a certain malty sweetness. Don't worry; it's perfectly normal. It would be unfair to characterize all Scottish caddies as I have just characterized them; however, it's totally fair to characterize them as recalcitrant yet funny, nimble yet slack, engaging yet disengaged (at times), friendly yet brusque, brutally honest yet heartfelt and helpful.

If you have a caddy, the best thing you can do is to take his or her advice; caddies usually know your game better than you simply by looking at you, looking at your clubs, and watching you warm up. If the caddy says take a 7-iron and hit to the left of the flag, take a 7-iron and hit to the left of the flag. The worst thing you can do is ignore the caddy's advice. Remember these two things also: (1) your caddy is likely betting on the outcome of your match, and (2) your caddy has not taken a course in customer appreciation or service from a customer service consultant or anyone else. And that is reason No. 243 that I love Scottish caddies.

Unless you spent your formative years in Scotland, you may encounter a bit of a language barrier in St. Andrews, especially with the caddies. They will understand you, but you will not always understand them. The root cause has more to do with phraseology than enunciation. Later in this book, there's a brief guide to key Scottish phrases, idioms, words, and sayings—at least the printable ones.

Once you know these, things will clear up. A bit. Just remember that everything said is in jest: the Scots are probably the funniest, wittiest, and most fun-loving people on the planet. And while they like to send it out, they will happily take it back.

You will never forget your first round at the home of golf. Make sure that you get a photo of you and your friends on the Swilcan Bridge at the eighteenth hole. Whereas most golf courses end up immediately adjacent to a clubhouse, it's the town that greets you as you finish up at St. Andrews. And that, too, is a welcome you will never forget.

Sea Island/The Cloister
Sea Island, Georgia
866.879.6238
www.seaisland.com

It's no secret that the South has been changing dramatically for the past three decades. Once quiet but now bustling cities such as Charlotte, Nashville, Atlanta, Birmingham, and Raleigh, among others, have been growing rapidly, eagerly welcoming newcomers not just from the United States but from all over the world. Is this the end of southern gentility, southern manners, and southern old-world charm? At Sea Island, the answer is a resounding *no*. What opened originally as a retreat for hard and true Old

South families now attracts a broader range of guests, including many from, get this, the *Northeast*. Yet, Sea Island has retained its loveliness and its southern-ness, and there is no clearer proof than the Avenue of Oaks, the archway of coastal trees that leads eager guests to Sea Island's many and varied attractions. It's straight out of a movie from the 1920s. After checking in, you almost expect Bobby Jones to greet you in the lobby, in a black tie, ready to meet friends at the bar before going to dinner. If you're looking for the best of the Old South and the accompanying relaxation of the coast, then there probably isn't a better place in the United States than Sea Island.

The ownership at Sea Island has not rested on its laurels. Beginning in the mid-1990s, the resort initiated a huge renovation program. One of the results? In December 2006, *Golf Digest* named Sea Island the top golf resort in North America.

Located on the Georgia coast exactly halfway between Savannah and Jacksonville, Sea Island comprises the Cloister, the Lodge, the Sea Island Cottages (at the beach), and three golf courses with impressive and even rare architectural backgrounds. The golf school boasts an impressive faculty. In addition, there's a spa plus some fine southern dining in some of the most ornate and unique dining rooms anywhere. For the nongolfer, a wide variety of activities is available—anything from fly fishing to riding.

Sea Island succeeds in part because it can welcome just about any type of guest. It's perfect for a wedding, for a foursome of hard-core golfers, for couples. It's perfect for extended families or for serious corporate meetings, for the person who loves golf and for the person who hates the game. But ultimately, Sea Island is perfect for the individual who wants to get away from it all and step back in time to a more civilized era. Hundreds of celebrities have stayed at Sea Island through the decades, mostly to get out of the limelight and kick back.

It all started, from a golf standpoint, in 1927 when the resort hired Walter Travis to design its first nine holes, which he routed through dense oak forest. Travis was the first American to win the British Amateur Championship, and he borrowed numerous architectural features from his links tours and brought them to Sea Island. Two years later, the finest British architects of the time, Harry Shapland Colt and Charles Allison, arrived to build the second nine. At Sea Island, they built some of the finest holes in the South.

Much has changed from a golf standpoint since Travis, Colt, and Allison finished their work. Tom Fazio rebuilt the Seaside Course in the late 1990s; it's located on the southern tip of St. Simon's Island and is seriously exposed to ocean winds. This was the course that Colt and Allison had originally designed. Rees Jones, Robert Trent Jones Jr.'s brother, rebuilt and augmented the Travis course. Jones's course is solid here; the architect clearly resisted the urge to plant his own style on the course, instead deferring to Travis's more minimalist original work. The newest course is the Retreat Course, which Sea Island resident and University of North Carolina alumnus Davis Love III designed. Most of Love's work is in the Southeast, and he has quietly built a solid portfolio of top-caliber courses that have more than held their own against top competition.

Sea Island's courses represent the finest in southeastern coastal golf and collectively provide the best possible introduction to this type of golf. The intelligent golfer will encounter large greens and small greens, plus mostly wide fairways often flanked by water hazards. The hazards vary in size and shape, but they provide key strategic interest in this flat part of the country. There are marshes and wetlands and narrow corridors through dense ancient oak forests. With a cooling breeze toward the end of a warm spring or fall day, it's almost impossible to beat the quality of this type of golf—especially at Sea Island.

For the walker, Sea Island is paradise. The resort encourages walking, and there are plenty of excellent caddies around. The distances from green to tee are usually minimal; an eager walker can easily play several days of thirty-six holes—especially during the summer months. The dense humidity and intense sun can make summer seem a bit much, but there are plenty of golfers and visitors who clearly enjoy Sea Island from June through August, especially families who head for the cottages and the complementary attractions at the beach. Fall and spring are the best times for golf at Sea Island, and winter is mostly comfortable even though there will be a few days when that thin 4-iron early in the morning will create bad vibrations that will rattle every vertebrae.

The three fine courses at Sea Island provide more than enough quality golf to satiate the serious intelligent golfer. But every golfer who visits Sea Island will benefit from a visit to its expansive Golf Learning Center. It's not the most imaginative name, perhaps, but the quality of the instruction is among the best of any golf school in the United States. The school boasts not just one *Golf Magazine* Top 100 Teacher but three. And each of those is a *Golf Digest* Top 50 Teacher to boot. It's rare at any golf school to find this level of accomplishment but certainly unusual at a smaller school at a resort destination. Augmenting the instruction are a fitness guru, a putting guru, and a mind guru. The school offers packages, clinics, and private lessons. A wonderful vacation would be to spend three days getting your game in shape then three days indulging in practical application.

After a day at the school or at one of the three courses, dining awaits in one of eight eateries. The big splurge at Sea Island is the private dining, an opportunity to host your own private dinner party in a room specially designed for that purpose. With notice, you get to book the room you want, then choose the menu and the wines. Why not the Georgian Private Dining Room with its handpainted mural and big center table? Or how about the Wine Cellar at the Cloister or the Wine Cellar at the Lodge? Over the years, Sea Island has amassed a significant wine collection that every serious oenophile should sample. There's fine dining at the Georgian Room, Colt & Alison, and 100 Hudson, but a more relaxed atmosphere at the Oak Room and the Davis Love Grill. Even if the pub is more your line of business, you should certainly enjoy the formality of dinner at one of the top restaurants at Sea Island. It's jacket and tie for men (and boys over twelve) in the fine dining restaurants.

Getting to Sea Island isn't difficult—and it's worth the effort. Jacksonville and Savannah airports have regular flights to airports all over the country; it's eighty miles from each airport. Those who want to get a little closer should try Brunswick Golden Isles, which is thirty miles to the west. The private McKinnon Airport is on St. Simon's Island close to the Cloister.

If it's your first time at Sea Island, the staff will treat you like you've been there before. That's because a significant number of people *have* been there before. Sea Island has a small army of regulars who return year after year, usually at the same time. In many instances, up to four generations of the same family have spent time at Sea Island. Many of the staff have worked at Sea Island for decades and are like friends. Guests routinely, sometimes not by accident, run into the same guests they have run into for years. It's a family affair.

Traditions are almost as important as family at Sea Island. There's bingo on Tuesday and Thursday evenings, and everyone gets dressed up. Guests have been asking for corn muffins and gold brick sundaes for generations. Dancing still takes place. There's an English certified dance instructor to help you with your steps—if you need to know how to waltz. The resort hosts special celebrations for special times, such as New Year's, Easter, and Thanksgiving.

Howard Coffin, born in 1873 and the founder of Sea Island, would surely be delighted with the current state of the resort. The recent $500 million total makeover has paid off. The seriously good golf ranks among the finest coastal golf in the country—east or west. The resort has the requisite five-star, five-diamond ratings, and there are now more than 500 guest rooms. But most important, Sea Island has retained its status as an enclave where manners, old-world charm, and the habit of standing when a lady enters the room or approaches the table still matter. For that alone, Sea Island is worth the price of admission.

KAPALUA RESORT
LAHAINA, MAUI, HAWAII
800.527.2582
WWW.KAPALUA.COM

For the past several years, the PGA Tour has started the long and winding road of its season at Kapalua. It's an invitation-only event featuring just the past winners from the previous season. Thus the field is always stellar, yet the galleries seem like the smallest in all of professional golf, primarily because the part of Maui that Kapalua occupies is extremely rural. For those millions watching the Tour from home, Kapalua must look like paradise with its shirt-sleeve temperatures, balmy breezes, and quiet acres of pineapple farms. Spectators and viewers also get a good look at the Plantation Course at Kapalua, perhaps the finest in all of Hawaii.

Kapalua, sitting on the northwestern tip of Maui, perfectly combines magnificent scenery, wonderful views, fine weather, and top-class golf. The resort offers two golf options: the Plantation Course and the Bay Course, which Arnold Palmer and Frank Duane designed. There's also the Hale Irwin-designed Kapalua Learning Center, perhaps the most beautiful golf school anywhere. Accommodations vary from the luxurious Ritz-Carlton Kapalua to elegantly appointed villas. For those who like it so much that they want a first or second home, Kapalua can even help you find a permanent property. In addition to golf, the resort's activities range from climbing to hanging around on one of the three beaches soaking up the sun in the most relaxed fashion possible.

The Plantation Course gets all the attention on television, but the Bay Course isn't exactly a poor sister. That should certainly be your thinking at the fifth, which has perhaps the best golf view at Kapalua. The preceding hole is a gambler that will tempt the big hitter to go for the green by cutting the dogleg. But it's tough to think clearly here—such is the intensity of the vista. Farther along, the par-4 sixteenth has a split fairway that offers you a choice between going left or right off the tee; it's not a long hole at 371 yards, so the more aggressive left-hand fairway will be very tempting even though it requires a career tee ball. The eighteenth is a big Arnold Palmer-style closer at 552 yards from the back tees. Two strong shots set up an approach to a shallow green surrounded by a moat of bunkers. The course recently undertook a restoration and re-grassing of many of the greens to improve playing conditions.

Even though the Bay Course is wonderful, it's the Plantation Course that's the star of the show at Kapalua. In addition to hosting the season-opening Mercedes Championship, the Plantation Course has also hosted LPGA events. This course can easily challenge the world's best, but the genius of its design is that the "average" intelligent golfer can enjoy it, and even if things are going really, really badly with the golf swing, the course has something that few courses offer: views of the sea from every hole.

Kapalua gave Plantation Course designers Bill Coore and Ben Crenshaw a large, natural, yet hilly site. Their main challenge was to incorporate the prevailing winds into the course's strategy. Coore and Crenshaw easily passed all the examinations, delivering, in 1991, a course that's very much Hawaiian yet radically different from any course in the state. Off the tee, the other course could not be more wide open. This helps the average intelligent golfer, especially when the trade winds are really howling. Anyone who manages to miss a fairway will lose a ball though; such is the density of the scrub and the length of the long grasses. The original site was large, about 240 acres, and Coore and Crenshaw clearly felt that the site and the routing needed big bunkers and big greens; the putting surfaces are among the largest anywhere.

The ingenious routing avoids ridiculous elevation changes or severely canted fairways while still offering some exciting downhill shots where the typically fast and firm conditions mean some fun. The approach shots to the seventh, eleventh, twelfth, and eighteenth holes are hugely enjoyable, especially the eighteenth, where the ball seems to tumble forever toward the green. It's one of the most exciting shots on the PGA Tour all year as the pros try to eagle this massively long par-5. Part of the challenge at Kapalua comes from the quirky and capricious greens, which are sewn with Bermuda grass. Most northern-tier courses have bentgrass, which is generally more predictable. Well-maintained Bermuda greens make for excellent putting surfaces, although grain (the direction in which the grass is growing) can grab the ball and send it sideways at the last moment. A downhill putt downgrain can be lightning fast, whereas an uphill putt going into the grain can be extremely slow. And the wind can blow so hard at Kapalua that it starts to affect the putts. There's nothing quite like standing over a four-footer wondering about the break and the grain while watching the ball oscillate.

If a good hearty walk through wonderful terrain is part of the attraction of golf for you, then you'll love the Plantation Course. Its hilliness makes for a good, solid, appetite-creating march, but along the way, you will get magnificent views of the ocean and will walk past natural vegetation and deep chasms. It's one of the most glorious settings for golf in all of Hawaii.

When it comes to pampering and living the good life, Hawaii is the type of place where each resort strives to out-luxuriate the other. At Kapalua, you'll find the pampering amenities to be among the best in the state. It all starts with where you decide to stay. The villas have one, two, or three bedrooms, and the Kapalua Golf Villas have luxury upgrades. Kapalua is one of the few resorts that offer full-sized homes as lodging options; the secluded luxury homes are located in the resort's neighborhoods. They would be excellent for a family, a large group, or a company retreat. If you want more of a hotel setting, then you're in luck. The Ritz-Carlton Kapalua recently finished a $125 million renovation. The hotel has 548 rooms and offers amazing sunset views over Molokai and Lanai—the islands next door. As befits a AAA Five-Diamond property, the hotel has twenty-four-hour concierge service and a host of amenities, including a spa.

The Ritz-Carlton and the main resort offer a wide variety of dining options. High above the resort, try the Plantation House at the Plantation Course Clubhouse. The restaurant, featuring Hawaiian Mediterranean cuisine, has won a number of local awards—try the New Zealand coldwater lobster tail. At the Ritz-Carlton, the top restaurant is the Banyan Tree, which offers what the resort calls "Asian-inspired" cuisine.

Some golf resorts are pretty much geared toward golfers. Some are perfect for couples, even if half of the equation doesn't play golf. Kapalua, however, is a resort that's perfect for the whole family. It features a full menu of organized children's activities ranging from junior golf clinics to snorkeling, art classes, and conservation tours.

Kapalua has three beaches and a host of on-campus and off-campus activities mostly for adults. The truly adventurous should try Kapalua Adventures, which offers all sorts of "extreme" sports such as flying down a zip line and going through a challenge course. It's guaranteed to get the blood pumping a little faster. That's ironic because the goal of Kapalua seems to be to get the blood pumping a little more *slowly*. The golf at Kapalua isn't do-or-die excitement. It's about options and strategy and soaking up the majestic views. It's about relaxing, decompressing, and enjoying the fresh seafood served almost immediately from the Pacific. That's why the season opener on the PGA Tour is great golf but almost seems anti-climactic. There's a lot of money on the line, but even the golfers at the top of the leader board seem totally laid-back. That is exactly the point at Kapalua.

CASA DE CAMPO
LA ROMANA, DOMINICAN REPUBLIC
800.877.3643
WWW.CASADECAMPO.COM.DO

The best non-tournament, non-championship TV golf program of all time is, without question, *Shell's Wonderful World of Golf*. The show started in the early 1960s, stopped in 1970, then took a long hiatus before returning in the mid-1990s. The show featured two famous golfers who would compete over eighteen holes at some exotic location or famous course. Even if the golfers weren't on the best form (which was rare), it was worth watching just for the location.

For example, one show took place at the ultra-private and mysterious Pine Valley, probably the best golf course in the world. The show's producers were serious globetrotters. They got as far as New Zealand, Scotland, and Kenya. Several shows took place in the Caribbean, and the golf was always fun to watch, but one thing was always clear: golf isn't the main attraction in this part of the world. The courses always looked ragged and poorly designed. Golf is an afterthought due to various factors, including lack of suitable land, cost, maintenance, and agronomic issues. Serious intelligent golfers simply seem to gravitate to more golf-centric traditional golf destinations.

But there's one spot in the Caribbean where golf is taken very, very seriously: Casa de Campo ("house in the country") in the Dominican Republic. Located on the island of Hispaniola, which it shares with Haiti, the Dominican Republic is easy to reach by air from any of the major airline hubs on the eastern seaboard. You can fly directly to Casa de Campo or to Las Americas International Airport in Santo Domingo, about eighty minutes from the resort. Casa de Campo features three golf courses, plus villas and apartments, fine dining, and a good variety of nongolf activities.

If golf really isn't your bag and you're looking for the textbook mega-Caribbean resort with all the fun, frolic, swimming pools, major beaches, and nightlife that lasts until dawn and beyond, look elsewhere.

Casa de Campo is much more relaxed and low-key, a family-friendly private and secluded resort. In 2004, *Travel + Leisure* rated Casa de Campo the best spot for families in the Caribbean. The resort has attracted an avalanche of media over the years, including mid-forties rankings in world golf course "best of" lists; it was No. 42 on the 2009 international ranking in *Golf Magazine*.

While many of the guests at Casa de Campo are there purely for the sun and lounging around, a significant number are serious intelligent golfers who couldn't care less for the Caribbean aspect and simply want to test themselves against a great Pete Dye course. The fact that Casa de Campo is in the middle of one of the Caribbean's finest destinations is simply a bonus. Fellow golf course architect and former Dye associate Tom Doak believes that the Teeth of the Dog Course at Casa de Campo is Dye's favorite son. Built in 1971, it's one of his earliest, and while Dye's current projects are first-rate, it's his early ones that are the most interesting and entertaining.

All three courses at Casa de Campo are Dye courses. The Dye Fore course (with perhaps the hokiest name in all of golf) is solid and boasts some excellent par-3s. The Links Course might have the most deceiving name in golf—it bears no relation to anything even vaguely linksy, but it's a fine course nonetheless until you get into the thick rough, which is almost inescapable. The Links Course actually has more of a parkland feel, wandering up above the polo fields and the pastures where the polo ponies graze.

The course that everyone wants to play is Teeth of the Dog, often referred to simply as Casa de Campo. The resort developers made the right decision when they handed over a big chunk of land to Dye and gave him pretty much *carte blanche*, a big budget, and no fewer than 300 laborers. Few, if any, architects get this sort of freedom and backing today. Dye found a wonderful piece of coastal property with a few miles of low coral cliffs; he even persuaded the ownership to reorient the entire resort around the site—a wise decision. To find the site, Dye scouted by air, boat, and off-road vehicle.

During the construction process, difficult due to the coral at the coastline, the laborers had to get good soil from a mile away from the course. Laborers used oxen to speed up the process. Construction took about eighteen months, and the result features seven holes seemingly right in the middle of the sea. The most photographed hole at Teeth of the Dog is the par-3 fifth, 155 yards from the back tees; it's the first hole right on the coast. The eighth has a tee built along a causeway so that the drive must be played pretty much from the middle of the water. Only Dye would come up with something that outrageous. The best holes on the course are the three on the back nine, beginning with the fifteenth, which plays along the cliffs. The sixteenth is a long par-3 over the sea to an oddly shaped green. The green on the seventeenth is perched along the coral cliffs. At certain times, on these three holes, the waves break onto golfers as they get ready to tee off.

From the back tees, the course is difficult—even for the best intelligent golfers. Teeth of the Dog, in 1974, hosted the World Amateur Team Championship; of the 590 rounds played, only three were under par. Unless you are a professional or top amateur—or totally crazy—play the course from the correct yardage, or you will soon feel like a dog has bitten you in the rear end, repeatedly. Casa de Campo offers a full cadre of caddies who know the course forwards and backwards. Employ one.

There's plenty at Casa de Campo for the nongolfer, including tennis, riding, fishing, skeet shooting, and shopping. There's even a VIP shuttle to a local casino in Santo Domingo. The highlight of the dining at Casa de Campo is an offshoot of New York's famous Le Cirque, called the Beach Club by Le Cirque. The resort offers several other dining options and also some fun entertainment in the form of a sports bar and a pub. La Cana Bar offers live entertainment with a local flavor.

The Casa de Campo visitor who undoubtedly needed those watering holes the most was a keen golfer from New York who originally planned a three-day visit. But he stayed a fourth day and then a fifth. When the director of golf asked the gentleman how long he was going to stay, the gentleman replied that he was going to stay long enough to hit one of the par-3s at the Teeth of the Dog with his first shot. According to Dye, in his autobiography *Bury Me in a Pot Bunker*, it took the man six days and a lot of sunburn before he finally bladed a 6-iron that ended up on the back fringe of the thirteenth. The man simply walked off the golf course at that point and headed for home.

Interestingly, when *Shell's Wonderful World of Golf* made a welcome return to the airwaves after its hiatus, one of the first matches took place at Casa de Campo. Fred Couples beat his golf mentor Ray Floyd. After the match, Floyd told the commentators that "Teeth of the Dog ranks with the great courses in the world." So if you want to spend some time in the Caribbean and you want really fine golf in a spot where there's plenty for the non-golfers to keep themselves occupied, you can't go wrong with Casa de Campo.

The Boulders Resort
Carefree, Arizona
888.579.2631
www.theboulders.com

Wouldn't it be fun to awaken Old Tom Morris from the dead and fly him (first class, of course) to Carefree, Arizona, to see the Boulders? What would he think about a place that looks like the surface of the moon, only rockier, and that somehow has two first-rate golf courses and a healthy number of golfers lining up to play them? What would he think about those thin ribbons of desert fairway? About the fortress greens with all their swales and movement? About those strange hut-looking things perched among the scrubby hills? What would Old Tom think about those crystal-clear skies and warm January days? The luxury and chef-driven restaurants nestled in among the silent cacti? A house with a working fireplace—in the desert?

My guess is that Old Tom Morris would love it all and be delighted that the game has grown to the point where serious people with serious money would actually build a golf course slap-bang in the middle of a desert and that serious people would then make the effort to play the course. Arizona would amaze Old Tom, just as it amazes any first-time visitor who cannot believe that grass grows and golf takes place in a world where it hardly ever rains, a world more suited to reptiles and carrion-seeking birds than golfers. The Boulders, like all the desert courses, is a testament to America's love for the game of golf and its ability to put anything pretty much anywhere, including what could easily pass as the perfect location for a spaghetti western.

The Boulders is located in the Sonoran Desert twenty miles north of Phoenix. While the resort says that it's in Scottsdale, it's technically in Carefree. The resort covers roughly 1,400 acres and comprises two golf courses, a school called the Boulders Golf Academy, a full range of luxury accommodations, the Golden Door Spa, tennis, six dining options, and boutique shopping.

Grass will always look strange in the desert, but the main lodge and all accommodations blend amazingly easily into the landscape. The Haciendas and Casitas are beautifully furnished. The intelligent golfer should try the Boulders Suite, with its living area, private patio, fireplace, and adjunctive amenities. If the suite is too much space for you, try a Sonoran Casita, which is perfect for a couple and also has a fireplace—along with wood-beamed ceilings, glazed Mexican tiles, and juniper wood.

There are two golf courses at the Boulders, the North Course and the South Course. Which is better, the North or the South? Both courses are top quality, so it's difficult to say which is definitively superior. This makes the Boulders something of a rarity. At most resorts, one of the courses is usually much better than the others; thus the resort has to work quite hard at times to persuade their guests to play the "inferior" courses. Though guests end up enjoying the "lesser courses," they always feel like they should be playing the star attraction. If there's a difference between the two courses at the Boulders, then the North might be slightly more demanding than the South, especially on the back nine.

How did the Boulders end up with two consistently good golf courses? In the beginning, there were just eighteen holes. When the resort wanted to expand its golf, they split the original eighteen and added new nines to each original nine. The same architect, Jay Morrish, designed both courses. And the resort clearly asked Morrish to make the courses mostly golfer-friendly. The most recent nine on the North Course is a little tougher than the others and perhaps has more visually striking holes than the South, but looks can be deceiving in golf; just because a golf hole looks good in a brochure does not necessarily mean that it's enjoyable for the average golfer.

The resort considers the fifth on the South Course its signature hole. A rock outcropping shelters the green on this par-5, and the hole offers some of the best views of the surrounding Sonoran Desert.

Big hitters hoping to go for the green in two take on some risk as the fairway narrows significantly close to the green, proving that the course has the brains to match the beauty. The fifth on the South Course isn't the only hole with a fine view; at the Boulders, this remarkable golf environment is omnipresent. In Southern California and Arizona, and even into Nevada and New Mexico, there's plenty of desert golf, but only the Boulders can boast this remarkable landscape. It's one of just a few resorts anywhere that has so seamlessly integrated its lodging and amenities into the surroundings.

Local laws allow only a set number of acres for each golf course. In more temperate areas, a course typically needs 150 to 175 acres. The Grove Park Inn in Asheville, North Carolina, has a fine golf course that sits on 125 acres, but that's a rarity. In the desert, golf courses are usually allowed only about ninety acres of turf. Thus the fairways seem like green targets set among the scrub, rocks, cacti, and desert. What happens if your ball leaves the oasis of green? Local rules vary from course to course. At many desert courses, the desert functions as a lateral hazard, which means you can drop a new ball at the point where the old ball left the green stuff. Penalty: one shot. Leaving the safety of the grass and wandering into the desert has its risks—prickly vegetation, strange creatures, strange *biting* creatures, difficult footing, dinged-up 5-irons. Courses change their local "desert" rules periodically, so when you get to the Boulders, check with the professionals in the golf shop about the way to treat the desert. The scorecard may provide the definitive answer also.

Mid-handicappers and relative newcomers to the game will want to play from the forward tees at the Boulders. But first-time visitors, if the course is not too busy, should take a few extra moments to take in the views from some of the back tees, one of which is only accessible by a spiral staircase. Many golf courses in excellent locations fail because the architect forgets that golf is supposed to be fun and that a golf course where all the par-3s, par-4s, and par-5s are roughly the same distance is guaranteed to bore the person who has made the effort to get to the excellent location. There's none of that at the Boulders. The intelligent golfer will find long par-4s and very short ones, long par-3s and some teeny ones, muscular par-5s and some that even a short hitter might think about reaching in two shots. Variety is the spice of life—and the lifeblood of great golf course architecture.

Once the golf adventure through the desert is complete, the Boulders hits an even higher gear. A visit to the Golden Door Spa (33,000 square feet) will soothe aches and pains. The menu at the spa goes well beyond what many other spas offer. There's a "Movement Studio" for the practice of yoga and Pilates (both good ideas for the intelligent golfer). Spa experts at the Boulders describe "The Labyrinth" as "a path to tranquility inspired by ancient Hopi medicine wheels." If that's not enough, try the Watsu, which promises an underwater "back-to-the-womb" experience. All this can happen before the more familiar visits to steam rooms, saunas, and Japanese baths. And if you want or need a basic massage or mud exfoliation, it's all here.

Service at the Boulders is top-notch, all the way from the expansive and well-stocked golf shop to the concierge staff, who can organize a good variety of off-campus activities, ranging from shopping to a cattle drive, Grand Canyon air tours, hot air balloon flights, rock climbing, and horseback riding. If there's a private course in the Phoenix area that you would like to play, the professionals in the golf shop might be able to help you get a tee time. A short hike from the resort leads to a rock shelf 400 feet above the golf courses that provides wonderful views not just of the resort but of the entire Phoenix area.

Donald Crawley, a *Golf Magazine* Top 100 instructor, is in charge at the Boulders Golf Academy. The school offers a full range of programs based around Crawley's "Golf Simplified" technique. With two courses at his disposal, Crawley and the staff of PGA and LPGA professionals can instruct on the course, which is always a bonus. The "Women to the Fore" program is a plan that all golf schools should offer; providing a lot of personal attention, it's specifically designed to help women who are new to the game feel at home on the golf course.

As long as the nongolfers in your party have survived the day intact and as long as the golfers in the group have not hit too many wild and crazy shots into the Sonoran Desert, you can all gather for the evening at one of the six watering holes and restaurants. For all-out mega indulgence, opt for Rusty's at the Boulders Club, which features steaks, fish, and pastas. For pre- or post-dinner drinks, head for the Discovery Lounge, with its fireplace and piano player Thursday through Saturday; there's a fine view of the waterfall, too. That's right—a waterfall in the desert. What would Old Tom think about that?

For those intelligent golfers from the northern-tier states who want golf instead of ice fishing in the cold and dark winter months, a golf trip in January, February, March, or April is a must. Many opt for South Florida, as the next section details, but why not head for the desert instead? Winter temperatures are mild, the sun shines almost incessantly, golf options are broad, and the scenery is sublime. If your golf travels take you to the Valley of the Sun, then spend a few days at the Boulders, where the golf is friendly and the setting is rare.

SOUTH FLORIDA DESTINATIONS

Most states or regions have a definitive No. 1 golf resort. In Oregon, it's now Bandon Dunes. In Wisconsin, it's Kohler. In North Carolina, it's Pinehurst. In South Carolina, it's Kiawah Island. But in Florida, which has close to 1,000 golf courses, there are plenty of candidates but no outright victor. So this section introduces several sumptuous resort destinations in South Florida that will provide the intelligent golfer with a home away from home.

When it comes to winter golf in the United States, the country is mostly split. Snowed-in golfers west of the Mississippi tend to head for the desert Southwest, while golfers east of the Mississippi tend to head for the Southeast. The big groups of pure golf maniacs often head for the neon and bawdiness of Myrtle Beach (and there's absolutely nothing wrong with that), while those in search of a more upscale, pampered, and relaxed atmosphere head for one of South Florida's epic golf enclaves. Of course, many of these are ultra-private and almost impossible for the nonmember to enjoy. Thankfully, there are plenty of options for the intelligent golfer who wants that type of privacy, service, and golf without necessarily moving to South Florida for the entire winter.

After a few days, though, you'll be sorely tempted to relocate for good. From Thanksgiving to Mother's

Day, typically, the sullen humidity seemingly evaporates, the daily thunderstorms of the summer months are rare, and calm breezes float in from the Atlantic and Gulf of Mexico. There's a reason that so many people from Connecticut, Vermont, Boston, Philadelphia, New York, and Philadelphia migrate to Florida for the winter.

So let's take a tour, shall we? We'll start on the Gulf Coast and end up on the Atlantic, but we'll take a purposefully circuitous route south, then east across the Everglades, then north from Miami. Got your golf gear? Got your eating and drinking boots? Let's go.

THE RITZ-CARLTON SARASOTA
SARASOTA, FLORIDA
941.309.2000
WWW.RITZCARLTON.COM

Situated on the highly grand North Tamiami Trail near downtown Sarasota facing Sarasota Bay, the Ritz-Carlton Sarasota is one of those larger-than-life hotels that would seem right at home in Miami, Los Angeles, or New York City. Reaching seemingly endlessly into the azure sky and built with plenty of marble and exotic materials, the hotel has a pinkish hue inside and out that highlights its luxuriance and style. It's relatively new, but inside you will feel like you're stepping into something straight from *The Great Gatsby*. It's that resplendent.

The Ritz-Carlton Sarasota is actually half residences and half luxury hotel rooms. All the rooms have wonderful views of Sarasota Bay, and all have a balcony. People who live on the property are essentially members of a club, which gives them access to such amenities as the spa, the beach club, and the golf course. The last two are off-campus. The Ritz-Carlton also organizes children's activities and offers several dining options, including one of the few Mobil Four-Star restaurants in South Florida, the Verona. Even the modest rooms are well appointed, and each includes a wonderful touch: an elegant writing table complete with hotel stationery. Now that's a throwback.

The Member's Golf Club at the Ritz-Carlton is a new course that Tom Fazio built on a former tomato farm and cattle ranch—typically flat Florida land. With this completely raw property, Fazio also created a somewhat typical Florida golf course with plenty of mounding and lots of water. But with a bigger budget and more time, Fazio created more undulation, and this provides the course with more character and interest than 95 percent of the other courses in the Sunshine State. At one point, the course reaches sixty-five feet. Hotel guests are automatically members of the golf course during their stay. You can take a cart if you'd like, or you can take a caddy. Or you can take a caddy and a cart. Whatever you choose, you'll find that the level of service and pampering is routinely wonderful. Everyone seems to know who you are as soon as you arrive.

Golf at the Ritz-Carlton Sarasota is a lot of fun. The fairways are wide, and there's no need to hit anything except the driver from all the par-4s and par-5s. Many of the holes have mounding that will steer a slightly off-line drive back to the middle. There's no need to worry too much about heavy rough; it's not part of the agenda. Remember, this is a resort course, and the intelligent golfer is there to have some fun. The greens are similarly large but have a lot of movement through subtle dips, swales, and ledges. Listen to your caddy to find the right portion of the green so that you minimize the chances of a three-putt, and maybe you can even make a birdie or two.

The longer holes are solid, yet it's the collection of par-3s that are the most impressive. The shortest from the regular tees is a modest 151 yards, but while the others are longer, they're not necessarily any harder. To help the mid-handicapper or novice golfer, most of the longer holes are open in front, which means that it's possible to run or bounce the ball in, an architectural feature that's somewhat rare on modern courses. Also rare is the self-containment; the course is a stand-alone with no houses or any sort of development—probably one of the many reasons that the course got into *Golf Magazine*'s Top Ten new courses the year it opened.

The new clubhouse is so opulent that it might keep you from rushing back to the mother ship. Sitting on one of the highest points of the property, the clubhouse overlooks the first, ninth, tenth, and eighteenth holes. The locker rooms have attendants, and there's outdoor seating under the trellises. There's also a grill, which serves a decent menu of golf favorites.

At the hotel, make a dinner reservation for Vernona, the aforementioned Mobil Four-Star restaurant. The cuisine is "regional organic," and the menu includes Key West Shrimp Ceviche with Heirloom Tomatoes, Avocado, and Baby Corn as an appetizer and Peanut-Chile Rubbed Australian Rack of Lamb for a main course. Featuring bright colors, plush seats, and big cutlery, Vernona's ambiance is old-school Florida.

Tampa Bay International Airport is well to the north of the Ritz-Carlton International, but Sarasota-Bradenton is a mere fifteen minutes from the property and has decent regional service to most eastern hub airports. The golf course is good enough to play it every day for a week without getting bored, but the Ritz-Carlton Sarasota is perhaps best for a quick hit-and-run extended weekend with some friends. If privacy, service, and ambiance are important to you, then you'll find them in spades at the Ritz-Carlton Sarasota.

THE RITZ-CARLTON GOLF RESORT, NAPLES
NAPLES, FLORIDA
239.593.2000
WWW.RITZCARLTON.COM

An easy drive down the coast from Sarasota, the original Gulf Coast Ritz-Carlton golf enclave is the Ritz-Carlton Golf Resort, Naples. Its sister property is the palatial Ritz-Carlton Naples just a few miles away, right next to the shore near downtown Naples. The setup provides plenty of options. You can stay at the Ritz-Carlton Naples and enjoy the golf at the golf resort, you can stay at the golf resort and enjoy the amenities of the hotel, or you can stay at the golf resort and totally ignore the Ritz-Carlton Naples. If someone in your party abhors golf, that person can hang out at the beach and enjoy the amenities while you enjoy the golf. Whatever your choice, you will find a highly relaxing golf break at the Ritz-Carlton and a superb level of pampering.

Let's go straight to the golf at the Ritz-Carlton Golf Resort, also known as the Tiburon Golf Club. In December 2007, the club hosted the Merrill Lynch Shootout, a postseason, two-person, betterball event that attracts many of the top players in the world. There are two courses, the Gold and the Black, both the work of Greg Norman and his design team. Norman hasn't built a vast number of golf courses, but the ones he has built have been solid architectural successes that have easily set themselves apart from the crowd. The reason? Norman has brought a number of the architectural features from the best Australian courses to America and added liberal doses of a Scottish theme—the stacked sod wall bunker. Instead of sand in the face of the bunker, there's grass or stacked layers of sod. Norman courses typically have generous fairways and no rough (you read that one correctly), yet a departure from the fairway usually means complete disaster as your ball will end up in thick overgrowth or swamp. It's a great combination that makes for enjoyable golf.

Tiburon Golf Club is a fully functioning golf club in its own right. The Gold and Black courses are open for resort play on alternate days. It might sound a hair complicated, but upon arrival at either the golf resort or the main resort, everything becomes much clearer; the friendly staff will orient you and get everything organized so that you should not have to lift a finger.

The front nine on the Black Course features the fascinating par-4 eighth, just 282 yards from the regular tees; it's followed by another great gambling hole, the par-5 ninth. The fourteenth is the most beautifully framed hole, but the hole that you'll remember the most, hopefully for all the right reasons, is the par-5 eighteenth, which features water running down the entire right-hand side. At 500 yards from the regular tees, it provides the opportunity for a closing birdie.

The Black Course ends with a par-5, and the Gold Course begins with one. A modest 475 yards from the regular tees, the hole provides an excellent birdie opportunity if you can navigate the interesting angles of attack. On the front nine, holes four and five hug a lake and are the most scenic holes on the course. On the back, the short par-4 thirteenth has beautifully designed waste areas flanking both sides of the fairway, but it's wide enough to tempt a smash with the driver to try to get it close to a green that's a mere 320 yards away. The seventeenth is an excellent example of a Greg Norman par-5 that presents a fascinating range of options; at just under 500 yards, it's the last realistic chance for a birdie before the tough eighteenth.

The Ritz-Carlton Golf Resort, Naples, does not have as many golf courses in its quiver as some resorts, but the two that it can access are as strong as any pair in Florida. Couple this with the service and the dining at both the golf resort and the main hotel, and it's a tough combination to beat. But just in case you want more golf during a longer trip, the concierge and the golf shop can help you get a tee time at some of the better private golf courses in the area—and there are plenty in the Naples area. Try Old Collier, a Tom Fazio design that hired caddies directly from Scotland.

If you're looking for quality instruction, the Ritz-Carlton Golf Resort, Naples, is the winter base of the Rick Smith Golf Academy. Smith is one of the top swing gurus in the country, and his staff includes numerous accomplished and experienced teachers. For group instruction, the school has a 2:1 student-to-teacher ratio, which is one of the lowest in the business.

Both Ritz-Carlton Naples properties offer a wealth of nongolf amenities and excellent dining. At the clubhouse of the golf resort, try Lemonia with its Tuscan cuisine and excellent views of the closing holes; if the weather is pleasant, there's alfresco dining. At the beach, try Artisans at the Beach, with its seafood bent; it's the only AAA Five-Diamond restaurant in southwest Florida. If you're more in the mood for a steakhouse, try the Grill, which offers the clubby feel of a classic steak house and features an excellent wine list.

The best gateway to the area is Southwest Florida International Airport, although Naples Municipal can handle most private aircraft. But why not take in both the Ritz-Carlton Naples and the Ritz-Carlton Sarasota? That's a week's worth of excellent golf, pampering, relaxation, and dining that a small golf group or a couple of couples would enjoy as part of a well-deserved winter break.

Now it's time to take the famous Alligator Alley across the Florida Everglades to Miami and its environs.

DORAL GOLF RESORT & SPA
MIAMI, FLORIDA
800.713.6725
WWW.DORALRESORT.COM

Doral is probably the most famous golf resort in Florida, for several reasons. First, it's been the home of a PGA Tour event for what seems like 900 years. Millions of viewers over the decades have tuned into to watch the drama at the eighteenth hole of its top course, the Blue Monster. Second, it has a golf course called . . . *the Blue Monster*. Third, Doral is the home of the flagship location of the top golf teaching institution in the country, the Jim McLean Golf School. That means Doral is on the Golf Channel at least once a month. And fourth, the resort and its five courses have hosted thousands of visitors since it first opened in 1962.

Now associated with Marriott, Doral is benefiting from a reinvestment program that is helping the resort maintain its status as one of Florida's top destinations. In addition to the golf courses, Doral has a spa and dining. But it's the meeting spaces that are the main attraction at the resort, with companies of all sizes coming to Doral for meetings and conferences. It's the lifeblood of the property, but not to the point where individuals, couples, and groups feel uncomfortable or unwanted if they are not wearing a nametag.

Part of the attraction for meeting planners is the proximity to Miami International Airport, the gateway to the Caribbean and South America for millions of travelers. At times, the proximity to MIA is all too apparent, especially when planes are landing on runway thirty. But that's Miami for you, and Doral is very much a Miami destination. This becomes evident as soon as you hop in a cab for the short drive to the resort. The driver will likely originate from Haiti or Cuba or another Caribbean country, and the language on the radio will be French or Spanish. Welcome to America's greatest multicultural city. Even the drive through the airport hinterlands and then through suburban and semi-industrial sprawl to the muted front gates of Doral pulsates with the vibrancy and power of this fascinating place. Once you reach that front entrance, everything becomes quieter and a bit more serene, which is exactly the goal, but at Doral, you are very much a part of this kaleidoscopic city.

Doral sits on a big piece of land, enough for its five courses. The Silver Course is slightly narrower than the other Doral courses and has an island green, the fourteenth. In 1999, it hosted the PGA Tour Qualifying School, generally a benchmark for quality and challenge. The Red Course requires brain more than brawn, especially with water on fourteen holes. It, too, is strong enough for professional play, having hosted the 2001 Office Depot Championship, an

LPGA event. Raymond Floyd lives in the Miami area and has designed several courses in South Florida. You can see his work at Doral's Gold Course. It's tight and narrow in spots, and the holes farthest from the clubhouse border tidy homes and apartments. Water comes into play on sixteen holes, and the mandatory island green is at the eighteenth, far and away the best hole on the course.

Greg Norman designed one of the most popular courses, the Great White, which has a completely different feel and look—a total departure for Doral. Flashy and bold, the Great White offers a tremendous test from the back tees on a windy day. In 2005, Doral tweaked the design, reorganizing the sixth and fifteenth, and planting native grasses. The course almost looks like it belongs in the Arizona desert. Instead of rough, Norman and his design team opted for tightly packed crushed coquina sand between the fairways. Norman also used pot bunkers throughout the property for strategic interest. And there's a triple green for the eleventh, thirteenth, and seventeenth. Whereas Doral's original courses have a little bit of a sameness to them, the Great White stands out—visually, as well as in play. The other courses are green; the Great White is just that—white. It's worth the trip to Doral for this course alone.

But the most famous course at this most famous resort in South Florida is the Blue Monster, the textbook big-time inland Florida golf course. The property could not be any flatter, so the interest comes from the water, the strategically placed bunkers, and the greens. The eighteenth is a long par-4 with water along the entire length of the left-hand side; the green is almost a peninsula and provides excellent entertainment for the spectators and the television viewers during the professional tournaments. The eighteenth is the best-known (most often featured on *SportsCenter*), but the Blue Monster has several other wonderful Florida holes. The par-5 tenth doglegs slowly around the lake that flanks the eighteenth and provides numerous permutations and angles of attack. The fourth is one of two long par-3s, and the twelfth is another excellent par-5 that seems to go on forever.

There are caddies at Doral, and you should certainly take one for the Blue Monster, which you will not enjoy if you end up in the seemingly light rough off the tee or choose the wrong set of tees for your ability. When you get to the eighteenth, check out the many and varied plaques commemorating the many and varied acts of golf heroism that have taken place on this storied course. Even if it's slightly beyond your ability, it's always fun to play a course that you have seen, or will see, on television.

A number of guests head off-campus for dining—many making the trek to super-trendy South Beach. But if you are unfamiliar with the area, you'll be fine at Doral, which offers plenty of dining. The most relaxing spot is Champions Bar and Grill, which has excellent bar food to complement the views of the Blue Monster's eighteenth hole. It's a great place for a group of intelligent golfers to relax.

Right next to the resort is the range, and at the far end of the range is the Jim McLean Golf School. At first appearance, it's not the most impressive-looking range, and there are plenty of golf schools in the United States with better facilities. But it's tough to find a golf school with a better and more accomplished faculty, headed by one of the world's top instructors, Jim McLean. One of the best reasons to visit Doral is to spend time with McLean and his staff. The school offers a palette of options, and you're highly likely to run into one of the numerous professional golfers who come to Doral for instruction. Unless you book a private session with McLean or take one of the six-day schools, you won't get a lesson with McLean himself, but don't worry—his top associates, called Lead Master Instructors, are first-rate.

Now that we're in the Miami area, it's time to head toward the beach, specifically Turnberry Isle.

THE FAIRMONT TURNBERRY ISLE
MIAMI, FLORIDA
866.840.8069
WWW.FAIRMONT.COM/TURNBERRYISLE

Located halfway between Miami Beach and Fort Lauderdale, the Fairmont Turnberry Isle Resort and Club is the type of property where movie stars and A-list celebrities will feel right at home. The broad, elegant, and expansive lobby features marble everywhere, and the adjoining rooms and lounges are beyond opulent. In a lounge, you might see Jack Nicholson, Billy Crystal, Burt Bacharach, Sir Ben Kingsley, or Whitney Houston, all of whom have stayed at Turnberry Isle. Located in Aventura, the resort occupies 300 acres. The property opened in 1970 but looks like it's been there a lot longer. That's because the centerpiece of Turnberry Isle, the Mediterranean-style hotel, has a turn-of-the-century feel and look that perfectly meshes with the older Miami hotels in and around South Beach.

Developer Dan Soffer was the creator of Turnberry Isle. He built the resort primarily as a business venture but also as a way to entertain his celebrity guests. He wanted to offer them privacy, as well as all the requisite amenities—including space for yachts. After the recent redesign of the golf courses, the powers-that-be renamed one of the golf courses after Soffer, a keen golfer.

The Fairmont portfolio of hotels and resorts includes some of the most palatial and luxurious properties in the world, including the Savoy in London, the Fairmont San Francisco, and the Plaza in New York City. Fairmont recently invested $100 million in Turnberry Isle, with clear results. The guest rooms and expansive suites are among the most sumptuous anywhere, and each room has a private balcony with wonderful views of what is, essentially, a quiet retreat in the middle of the hustle and bustle of Miami's northern reaches.

Some of that $100 million went into a total renovation of the two golf courses, the Soffer and the Miller. Ray Floyd essentially blew up the old courses to start again and reorganized the driving range and practice facilities. The work also included extensive landscaping—so the courses have the classic South Florida look, with palm trees and deep green Bermuda grass. Few people think of waterfalls and Miami in the same sentence, but the courses feature several of the former, including one that cascades a full sixty-four feet. Turnberry Isle hosts a postseason professional skills challenge and an LPGA event, the Stanford International Pro Am.

The professional events take place on the Soffer Course, which was formerly the South Course. The former Robert Trent Jones Sr. courses at Turnberry Isle weren't exactly lower-tier courses, but they were mostly flat, and one of Floyd's goals was to give the fairway some movement and undulation. Ditto with the greens. The other goals were to improve the playability for the resort guest by widening the fairways and to improve the fun for the intelligent golfer by providing options and different angles of attack. The par-71 Soffer Course is longer and more challenging than the par-70 Miller course. The one holdover from the original design is the long and wonderful eighteenth, with its island green in full view of the hotel.

The Miller Course is slightly shorter; its defining feature is the Boros, a large body of water named for Julius Boros, the famous golfer who loved nothing more than golf and fishing. In the middle of the lake is a new "Flamingo Island" that's home to the resort's pink birds; it's a safe spot for them to nest. There's even space set aside for a bird refuge.

With all the temptations in and around Turnberry Isle, especially those a little farther south, it seems almost mandatory to head off-campus for some extracurricular fun and frolicking. Nevertheless, the resort has worked hard to keep you near the comfort and sanctuary of your room or suite—first with the wonderful Ocean Club Bar after golf, where the intelligent golfer will appreciate that a resort this upscale does not think itself too haughty to serve a hamburger. For drinks before dinner, head for the

Cascata Grille and Bar or simply enjoy a drink in the resort's lounge. The former is formal enough for that pre-dinner drink yet relaxed enough to enjoy a sporting event on the television. Fairmont has also invested in its dining, specifically its Cascata Grille, whose Mediterranean cuisine primarily uses local seafood and seasonal produce.

At any eatery or watering hole you choose at Turnberry Isle, you might not necessarily be sitting next to a movie star, sports star, captain of industry, or television personality, but you will certainly experience the luxury, privacy, and old-school Miami-ness that keeps the resort's loyal guests coming back. For pure opulence with some fine golf, all recently restored and rejuvenated, it's tough to beat Turnberry Isle.

But let's head a little farther up the coast to the grandmother of them all, Boca Raton Resort.

BOCA RATON RESORT AND CLUB
BOCA RATON, FLORIDA
888.543.1277
WWW.BOCARESORT.COM

In the travel and leisure industry, perhaps the most overused word is *iconic*. Even a modern hotel of no great stature, interest, or substance can be iconic, and so too can its spa, golf courses, and sports bar. But one resort that absolutely and definitely qualifies as iconic is the Boca Raton Resort and Club a few miles north of Fort Lauderdale.

The resort comprises two golf courses, the main hotel (the Cloister), the Yacht Club, the aptly named Tower, the Boca Bungalows, dining, extensive conference facilities, a spa, thirty tennis courts, six swimming pools, fishing, plus a half-mile of private beach. Given all that, you know that Boca Raton isn't exactly a retreat or quiet enclave, but it's a wonderful spot nonetheless—and perfect if you are looking for a more energetic golf getaway that an entire family, from the youngest toddler to the oldest grandmother, could enjoy. A new ownership group took over in 2005 and has been reinvigorating the resort with a massive reinvestment and improvement program. One of the goals is to attract a younger, upscale family crowd, which will only add to the vibrancy of the resort. Boca Raton is also a prime conference and meetings facility, so the intelligent golfer is highly likely to run into clusters of people wearing nametags that begin, "Hello, my name is . . . " Corporate groups are the lifeblood of places such as Boca Raton Resort, and those groups add to the ambiance once their business is over and it's time for some pleasure.

Everything began at Boca Raton Resort when architect Addison Mizner eyed a piece of property well to the south of a development in Palm Beach. Mizner and his group eventually acquired a whopping 17,500 acres with the goal of creating the greatest resort in the world. When the main hotel property, the Cloister, opened in 1926, it quickly attracted royalty and corporate titans. The glory lasted only a season, though, as the resort's economic backing began to falter. But Mizner had succeeded in building one of the most remarkable pieces of pre-war Florida decadence, and today the Cloister stands as a testament to his vision and architectural eccentricities.

Since the Roaring Twenties, the resort has weathered both hurricanes and a number of different owners, most of whom, to be fair, have been dedicated to preserving the resort's status as one of Florida's top vacation destinations. It's certainly one of the largest now, with more than 1,000 rooms, suites, and bungalows. But the intelligent golfer should still try to stay at the Cloister if at all possible, especially if he or she is traveling with a group of fellow intelligent golfers. The drive to the original hotel down Camino Real is one of the greatest resort entrances in the United States.

If you are with the family, opt for a suite or one of the bungalows. The children will want to take advantage of the beach, but if they want a more structured environment or if you want to get to the golf courses feeling that the little ones will be happy all day, Boca Raton offers Camp Boca, which is split into two groups: Boca Tots for ages three to five and Boca Bunch for ages six to eleven. If the teenagers have been watching *Caddyshack*, you can tell them that the producers shot the

Fourth of July dinner-dance scene at the resort.

Part of the golf lore at Boca Raton includes legendary professional and teacher Tommy Armour, who worked with his pupils from beneath the shade of an umbrella. They were in the sun, he was in the shade, and the story is that Armour almost always had libation within easy reach. There is surely many a professional golf instructor today who would love to emulate the Scot in this regard. Sam Snead, who won several major tournaments in his excellent career, was Boca Raton's director of golf from 1955 to 1969.

The two golf courses are called the Resort Course and the Country Club Course. The former is right next to the Cloister and has a large clubhouse that includes a steakhouse restaurant. The latter is off-campus but only a short drive away. The Resort Course, originally built by William Flynn in 1926, is one of the oldest courses in Florida. It's not a long course by modern standards, and it boasts tons of character. The Country Club Course opened in 1984. This longer and more modern course is home to short-game schools organized by short-game specialist instructor Dave Pelz. The Country Club's best hole, with its island green, might be the eighteenth.

After golf, yachting, pampering at the spa, or hanging out at the beach, the resort offers plenty of dining options. The Homestead, a steak house, unashamedly serves huge portions of everything. Chef Angela

Hartnett is the guiding force behind Cielo, on the top floor of the resort's tower. Hartnett describes the cuisine as "continental with an Italian flair." For a true indulgence, reserve the Chef's Table for six to ten people; the private area overlooks the kitchen, and guests get a seven-course meal with Hartnett herself describing each course. The Chef's Table option proves that Boca Raton is able to remain civilized while still catering to a large number of guests. Further proof comes in, or at, the Cathedral in the Cloister. Open for breakfast only, it provides a glimpse of the past at Boca Raton with its vaulted ceilings, picture windows, and intricate stonework. It's a great place to start the day.

Boca Raton strives to offer the service and attention of a much smaller hotel within the framework of this magnificent and storied property. As such, it has a certain elasticity that other resorts cannot offer: you can go to Boca Raton Resort as a family, a company group, a group of golf buddies, or just as a couple. In each instance, you'll likely find a way to enjoy yourself in an intelligent fashion on or off the golf course. But will you find it to be *iconic*? That's up to you and your sense of history.

Our tour is nearly complete. It's time to head to perhaps the most famous *and* infamous of all Florida cities, Palm Beach. It's time to investigate another Florida property, the Breakers. Believe it or not, it predates Boca Raton.

THE BREAKERS PALM BEACH
PALM BEACH, FLORIDA
888.273.2537
WWW.THEBREAKERS.COM

The first incarnation of the Breakers opened in 1895. It burned to the ground. The second incarnation of the Breakers opened around 1904; it, too, burned to the ground. It took less than a year to build the Breakers that you see today, a massive but elegant and beautiful—and mostly self-contained—hotel right on the beach. In fact, the Breakers seems to be located right in the middle of the azure Atlantic. Architect Leonard Schultze had obviously been to Italy a few times. The Breakers is an Italian building on steroids, maxed out with every conceivable Italian architectural feature. The lobby and entrance areas are reminiscent of the Great Hall of the Palazzo Carega (circa 1560) in Genoa. The exterior and its surroundings are impressive enough, but the interior is even more jaw-dropping.

Like the other resorts on our tour, the Breakers has all the requisite amenities: golf, restaurants, rooms (550 of them), a long list of accolades and awards, children's activities, a spa, and the beach club. But the Breakers goes one step beyond with a mini-shopping village featuring top retailers. The Breakers also has AAA Five-Diamond status. Its staff of 2,300 is fluent in more than fifty languages. Floors six and seven are part of a special club where the already mega-pampered guests get even more pampering, including afternoon tea. The fitness center has ocean views. The top restaurant has one of the top wine cellars in Florida. The resort even runs an off-site restaurant in the heart of Palm Beach. At the beginning of this section, I said that there might not be a definitive resort in South Florida. If I had to correct that statement, under some type of duress, my nod would go to the Breakers—truly, the ultimate luxury resort.

But let's get to the hard-core details for the hard-core intelligent golfer. The off-campus golf course is the Breakers Rees Jones Course, just a short ride from the main hotel. Originally designed by Willard Byrd and updated by Joe Lee, who designed a vast number of Florida golf courses, the Breakers contracted, as the name of the course indicates, Rees Jones to redesign the course. Consistent with Jones's courses elsewhere, the Breakers Rees Jones Course is generous for the most part off the tee, which is fair given the breezes that frequent the area. The par-5 sixth, however, narrows toward the peninsula green that juts precariously out into the water. This course often requires heroism, especially on the par-3s where shots that don't make it all the way to the green complex will find a watery grave. Is it as friendly to the resort guest as other Florida resort courses? You'll have to be the judge.

Thankfully, the Ocean Course is different. Whereas original Rees Jones courses are modern with a capital M, the Ocean Course is old-school. In fact, it's the oldest eighteen-hole golf course in Florida that's still in use. But today's Ocean Course bears no relation to the one that opened in 1897. For starters, Donald Ross redesigned it in the 1920s. In 2000, Brian Silva, who has successfully updated several Ross courses, gave the Ocean Course a much-needed facial. The big hitter may want to head to the Rees Jones course, though; the Ocean Course is much more about fun than muscularity.

Several par-4s are short-ish, and most intelligent golfers will approach these holes with a wedge or short iron. The key to scoring well is avoiding the ornery bunkers that flank the fairways. Once safely organized off the tee, club selection is particularly important. Water quarters into some of the greens, so anything short might find the hazard; putts from above the hole are no picnic, especially when the greens are fast. Ross believed in lengthy par-3s, and the course provides a couple of good examples, especially on the back nine: the thirteenth is 221 yards from the back tees, and the sixteenth is 212 yards, this time with water to the right of the green. The eighteenth is right next to the front entrance, and the hotel, with its two towers, is always in view on any of the holes.

If your round has gone really well at the Ocean Course, you'll be thinking about a way to celebrate in the hotel. The flagship restaurant at the Breakers is L'Escalier; this most formal of the eateries serves contemporary French cuisine with highly stylized presentation. There's also a champagne trolley. The less-formal Brasserie L'Escalier offers French bistro fare. Both restaurants have a superb wine list, easily one of the best in Florida, with more than 1,400 selections from a wine cellar with around 25,000 bottles. The resort has a Master Sommelier, Virginia Philip, to assist with the selections. Philip is one of the top wine experts in the country. Perhaps the most intriguing restaurant at the Breakers is Echo, which lies off-campus in the center of Palm Beach. Echo specializes in contemporary Asian cuisine. For Sunday brunch, try the Circle, with its ornate frescos on the ceiling. For pre-dinner drinks, the Tapestry Bar is a must. Fifteenth-century tapestries frame the room, and antique mirrors give it a grandeur that befits the resort. The menu is cocktails and caviar.

The Breakers isn't a yuk-it-up place with sawdust and peanuts on the floor; thus it's not the best destination for golfers who want to golf hard and play even harder. But for four to eight golfers looking for the ultimate in Palm Beach-ness, the Breakers is the perfect location, especially if you have connections at some of the ultra-private courses in the vicinity. While the golf at the Break-ers is fine, it's even better at certain spots well away from the compound.

With on-site organized activities, the child-friendly Breakers is perfect for a family. But perhaps where this resort works best is for a couple, a couple of couples, or a small group of friends, some of whom play golf, some of whom enjoy spas and serious shopping.

Whatever the size or inclination of you and your group, you'll find that the Breakers is one of the most beautiful resorts in America and the perfect spot for a well-deserved few days of subtle indulgence.

 # LONDON DESTINATIONS

Most intelligent golfers from North America who visit the British Isles to golf opt for Scotland or Ireland. Sometimes it's heritage. Sometimes it's a desire to see and play the courses that routinely hold the Open Championship—wonderful and historic places such as Royal Troon, Muirfield, and Carnoustie. Sometimes it's the totally understandable desire to get to the birthplace of golf and experience the pure joy (and the sheer penury) of links golf. Every intelligent golfer should make the effort to play at least a few of the early links courses in Scotland or Ireland at least once. Think of it as a sacred responsibility.

Which country is better, Scotland or Ireland? Heritage, again, may play a part in this debate. If your name is Iain Campbell, then you'll lean toward Scotland. If your name is Shamus Daley, you'll lean toward Ireland. Maybe. Those who have been to both countries extensively but have no firm roots in either are somewhat split. If you are one of the fortunate few who has played golf in Scotland *and* Ireland, or even if you aren't yet, let me suggest a third possibility that you should definitely consider: London.

In the mid-1700s, when golf started to become slightly more popular in Scotland and early golf clubs began to formulate the rules of the game, golf began its global emigration by slowly moving into the common areas around London. There's evidence of golf in London before Victorian times, but it was during the mid- to late nineteenth century that golf started to take root permanently. Coastal sites to the south and east of London were the first candidates for expansion— until the first serious golfers discovered a sandy belt of soil extending for several miles in a wide crescent roughly from what is now Heathrow Airport, directly west of London, to Gatwick Airport, directly south of London. Geologists call this anomaly bagshot sand. But it's better known to intelligent golfers as heath-land, and the best courses around London are called neither *links* courses nor *parkland* courses. They are called *heathland* courses, and collectively, they comprise some of the finest golf courses anywhere.

Let me go out on a limb here. If you placed Pinehurst No. 2 in the middle of the heathland courses, nobody would pay it much attention. Conversely, if you plucked one of the heathland courses and plopped it down, foliage and all, somewhere near New York City, it would likely be one of the very best courses, if not *the* best. And if you think I'm crazy, look at the world rankings in the big golf magazines and you'll see some of the courses I'm about to mention. Many are already right up there, and others are finally getting on the radar screen and ascending the rankings—primarily through word of mouth. If any of the major heathland courses were on television more or made an effort to attract the golf course raters and the golf writers, then you would know a lot more about them. But these are private clubs, not resorts striving to fill rooms and tee sheets. The members at these clubs know what they have, and they don't need a magazine ranking to tell them that their course is something seriously special.

A large part of the appeal comes from the beauty and uniqueness of heathland. The sandy soil makes for near-perfect turf year-round; it's often playable in winter and even after significant rain. Other courses in London, situated on thick clay, are typically too muddy from November to late April for serious golf. And if the summer is dry, the clay-based courses become rock hard and almost too bouncy—sort of like playing golf with a superball. Heathland is often wooded, usually with beautiful birch, horse chestnut, oaks, and sometimes fir and pine. Bright green ferns also grow in abundance, and many courses, in lieu of thick grass, have stands of heather defining the fairways. Add to this just a hint of wildness plus the perfect topography, and you have the best possible land for inland golf in the United Kingdom.

When the serious clubs began to establish golf courses in the early years of the twentieth century, they were extremely fortunate to have the services of some world-renowned architects at their disposal.

Chief among these was Harry Shapland Colt. He remains not particularly well-known in North America even though one of his few designs in the United States happens to be Pine Valley, generally thought of as America's best course, or at least one of its top three. And Pine Valley wasn't even his best work. So when you think of the heathland courses, think of something even better than America's best. Yes, these courses are that good.

Other architects active in this period were Alister MacKenzie, who designed Cypress Point, and James Braid, who designed many of England's finest courses. Sir Guy Campbell, another prolific golf architect, was also around at the time. Colt and the others could not move much dirt or land when they were building these courses. Since they had to go with the land as it lay for the most part, each of the heathland courses has its blind or semi-blind shots, its quirks, and the occasional hole that looks or feels awkward or even slightly out of place. A golf architect today wouldn't tolerate this, yet the "black sheep" holes add character and interest and only make the golf that much better. Don't expect the "standard" par-72 configuration with four par-3s, four par-5s, and ten par-4s. Again, going with the land and the available space, one heathland course might be a par-69 with just one par-5, while another might have five par-3s, including a pair back to back. There might be a string of eight par-4s in a row, or there might be a par-5 that's just a fraction longer than a par-4. There's nothing cookie cutter about English golf.

A trip to the heathland courses is best suited to a small and fast-moving group of two to four golfers. The beauty of a trip to London is that nongolfers will never be able to complain. You should choose a hotel in a location central to the heathland courses (Windsor would be perfect), yet close to a railway station. In the morning, while you and your group head for the golf course, the others can catch a train into London.

The London area has its resorts, many of which offer excellent golf, with top-notch hotels and amenities very much in the American mold. But none of them offers the heathland option or anything really close. And few golf tour specialists really know the situation in and around London; even when they do, their itineraries miss some of the true gems. To get to some of these top courses, the intelligent golfer must go it alone—and write some of the most charming letters ever written. Yes, it's old-fashioned, but that's the way it is, even in the age of e-mail and satellites. More on how to write those letters follow in this chapter. First, however, here are the courses you should target.

ORGANIZING YOUR HEATHLAND TRIP

*I*f you want to stay at the Breakers Palm Beach or Pebble Beach in the United States, life is relatively easy—by design. You call up. You speak with a friendly reservations specialist. You organize a flight or alternative travel. You arrive. You have a vacation. You leave. All you really had to do was get there. It's not so easy, unfortunately, on the heathland courses. You must organize your own hotel stays and book all the golf yourself. It's possible that the person who organized your tour to Scotland or Ireland could help with a hotel, but organizing the golf may prove too difficult. Still, it's not as hard as it sounds. Here are the steps you should take:

ONE: *Choose your dates*—well ahead of time. The optimum window is May to October, although May and September to mid-October are the best times to visit as there are not as many tourists around and the courses will have more time available for visitors. Plan several months in advance; nonmember days quickly book up at some courses.

TWO: *Choose your group*—carefully. Heathland golf is best for slightly better than average golfers (and above) who like to walk, appreciate the history of the game, and will be on their best behavior.

THREE: *Get out your pen and write to the Secretary.* In the United States, a secretary is an administrative assistant. In the United Kingdom, at a golf club, *the Secretary* is the person who runs the club and is usually more important than the president, usually called "the Captain." A letter like the one below should

suffice. It can be on your personal or your business letterhead. But do not send a fax, and do not send e-mail.

D.G. Smythe Esq.
The Secretary
The Heathland Golf Club
Upper Bagshot
Berkshire XO1 B52
England

Dear Mr. Smythe,

In the first week of October 2013, I am planning a golf tour to the heathland courses west and south of London. My group includes myself and two others. Our USGA handicaps are 9, 13, and 6, respectively. We are members of the Midland Dunes Country Club in Podunk, Ohio.

We would very much like to play The Heathland as part of our trip. The best days for us would be the fifth or the sixth, but we have some flexibility. We would like to play both the North and South courses, if that's possible, and if you have members who would enjoy a match with us, all the better. We will, of course, reciprocate in Podunk.

The best way to reach me is through e-mail at the address below. If it's possible for us to visit The Heathland, please let me know about any fees, which I will forward well in advance of our arrival.

Thank you for your consideration and assistance, and I look forward to your reply.

Sincerely,

Thomas Milton

Thomas Milton

The Secretary will likely reply via e-mail, and your correspondence can go back and forth digitally from this point forward. Still, it will behoove you to be formal even in your e-mail correspondence.

FOUR: *Book your flights.* Heathrow is best for most of the heathland courses, but Gatwick is fine.

FIVE: *Book your hotel.* See or call a travel agent who knows something about that part of the world. The Secretary with whom you are corresponding via e-mail will know some good hotels.

SIX: *Arrange travel.* You can book a rental car, but the easiest way to get around will be by private taxi or minivan—with a driver. The hotel can help you find a reputable company. Navigating in this part of the world is very tricky, and the entrances to many of the clubs are almost impossible to find. And everyone drives on the left side of the road.

SEVEN: *Read up.* There are lots of good books about the heathland courses, and you will enjoy the experience more if you know something about the courses. Some general notes about London golf:

✦ Many courses are two-ball courses all or most of the time. This means that you can play match play only if there are two of you. If there are four in your group, you will have to play foursomes (alternate shot).

✦ Bring a jacket and tie, and have both with you at all times.

✦ Change your shoes in the locker room.

✦ Change back to your nongolf shoes before entering any of the nongolf areas such as the bar or the dining room.

✦ If you win the bet, buy the first round of drinks.

✦ People in the United Kingdom drink in "rounds." When it's your turn to buy the drinks, it's "Your shout" and don't wait until someone asks. When you notice that everyone is a bit low, ask "What's yours?" of the group.

✦ You are going to walk. Some courses have trolleys (pull-carts), but very few have buggies (carts). Get in shape, as some of the courses are hilly.

✦ The best guidebook to the United Kingdom is *The Good Beer Guide*.

✦ Most pubs and restaurants stop serving food at around 9 p.m.

It's unlikely, of course, that *everything* will go smoothly, and it's highly unlikely that you'll get a week without some rain. But for the industrious and the adventurous intelligent golfer, a golf trip to London will provide exposure to some of the finest inland golf on the planet. You will also get to know, if you are open and friendly, some of the most intelligent and sporty golfers you will ever meet.

SWINLEY FOREST GOLF CLUB
SOUTH ASCOT, BERKSHIRE, ENGLAND
+44.0.1344.874.979
E-MAIL: SWINLEYFGC@AOL.COM

Colt described this as "his least bad course," which means that it's the best that Colt ever designed—there are quite a few golf architecture critics, armchair and otherwise, who think the same. The first hole and the last hole, both visible from the beautiful clubhouse, are not of the highest quality, and this can be hugely misleading. But once you're in the forest beginning at the second hole, it's one great shot after another, all in the most idyllic, peaceful, and majestic setting imaginable, with massive rhododendron bushes often providing beauty and hazard in equal measure. The course hosts company days (small corporate outings) periodically, but there's a strong likelihood that you'll have the whole place to yourselves. The course might well have the best set of par-3s of any of the heathland courses, and that's saying something. If there is just one course in this magical area that you play, play this one.

THE BERKSHIRE GOLF CLUB
ASCOT, BERKSHIRE, ENGLAND
+44.0.1344.622.351
WWW.THEBERKSHIRE.CO.UK

The two courses at the Berkshire Golf Club include plenty of holes by Harry Shapland Colt, and there's also the work of Herbert Fowler and Tom Simpson, both of whom were excellent architects in their own right. The Red Course is the stronger of the two, with six par-3s, six par-4s, and six par-5s. The Blue Course begins with a soul-searching long par-3 that will wake you up if you have stayed too long at lunch and had one too many pints.

ROYAL ASHDOWN FOREST GOLF CLUB
FOREST ROW, EAST SUSSEX, ENGLAND
+44.0.1342.822.247
WWW.ROYALASHDOWN.CO.UK

A true lay-of-the-land course built in 1891 and mostly unchanged, this hilly course offers lovely, peaceful views from the higher holes. By law, because the course lies in the middle of Crown Property, there can be no bunkers. But there's plenty of heather and other natural obstacles. Because the architect did not move anything at Royal Ashdown, the course has its quirks, like the crossover at the first and the eighteenth.

The best way for any intelligent golfer to beat jet lag is to get straight off the plane and play golf. Royal Ashdown is about twenty minutes by car from Gatwick. And after that, visit the simple but very welcoming bar, just a few benches around the exterior of a small room.

ST. GEORGE'S HILL GOLF CLUB
WEYBRIDGE, SURREY, ENGLAND
+44.0.1932.847.758
WWW.STGEORGESHILLGOLFCLUB.CO.UK

With twenty-seven excellent holes, St. George's Hill provides the textbook example of first-rate heathland golf. The clubhouse, perched seemingly impossibly on a hillside, is one of the most imposing you'll see anywhere. Inside, it's pure English golf, with gilded names on boards listing the winners of past tournaments and hardwood paneling everywhere. As at Swinley, the first hole is not the best, but the quality of the course improves significantly and stays that way all the way around. Even the additional nine is rock solid.

Sunningdale Golf Club
Sunningdale, Berkshire, England
+44.0.1344.621.681
www.sunningdale-golfclub.co.uk

There are two courses here, the Old and the New, even though the New isn't really new anymore: it dates to 1922. Harry Colt designed this one and revised the Old. Both courses are so strong, yet different, that it's impossible to say which is better. Both occupy prime heathland near Windsor. Several of the big boys of European golf play here regularly. And Sunningdale's membership includes some of the most successful businessmen in the United Kingdom, in addition to several members whose families began the club. The membership is welcoming, and the best way to enjoy Sunningdale is golf in the morning, lunch in the clubhouse, then golf in the afternoon. There isn't a better thirty-six-hole day anywhere. And the best part of the day will likely be the halfway hut at the only point in the middle of the property where the two nines meet. There, you will find the most perfect English sausages. Take a minute to view the gallery of famous people who have visited this little piece of heaven.

Perhaps the greens on the New are more difficult, and the Old offers a bit more width off the tee, but both courses are among the very best not just in

England but in the world. Late in the day, on a warm, sunny afternoon, the view from the seventeenth fairway on the Old Course—toward the broad open expanse of land in front of the clubhouse and the large specimen tree that shelters the eighteenth green—is a sight you will never forget.

WALTON HEATH GOLF CLUB
TADWORTH, SURREY, ENGLAND
+44.0.1737.812.060
WWW.WALTONHEATH.COM

Like Sunningdale, Walton Heath has an Old Course and a New Course, both of which are almost 100 years old. The Old is a fine course with a number of serious holes; it has some of the toughest heather of any heathland course. The problem with the wiry heather is that a good lie is really a bad lie, and what looks like a bad lie is often a good lie. So admire the heather, but avoid it at all costs; it can turn a good golfer into a hacker very quickly. Perhaps the New Course isn't as good as the Old Course, but the two still make for a great day. Both courses are more than 7,000 yards from the tips and thus provide a test for the longer hitter, who might find some of the other heathland courses a hair too short. Walton Heath is also a former Ryder Cup venue.

Woking Golf Club
Woking, Surrey, England
+44.0.1483.760.053
WWW.WOKINGGOLFCLUB.CO.UK

A quiet and venerable club with a wonderful history that dates to 1893, Woking is not a long course, but there are still some long and testing holes, including the par-3 second at 200 yards and the par-5 fourteenth that, given some fast and firm conditions, could be reached in two shots. The green is directly in front of the part of the clubhouse where members tend to congregate for refreshment; thus, it's the perfect spot to showcase your talents to a small gallery.

Wentworth Club
Virginia Water, Surrey, England
+44.0.1344.842.201
WWW.WENTWORTHCLUB.COM

If you have ever watched the World Match Play Championship, an event that's had a variety of sponsors over the years, then you might have seen golf at Wentworth, perhaps the most corporate of all the heathland clubs. The West Course, called "The Burma Road" due to its length, is a good test for the professional yet still fun for the average player. The East Course is more endearing and friendlier than its austere sibling. Wentworth is generally busier than the other heathland courses. Note the white and ivy-colored clubhouse, which looks like a small castle. There's a newer course, the Edinburgh, that could also be part of your itinerary.

WEST SUSSEX GOLF CLUB
PULBOROUGH, WEST SUSSEX, ENGLAND
+44.0.1798.872.563
WWW.WESTSUSSEXGOLF.CO.UK

The most southerly, perhaps, of the heathland courses, West Sussex is also the most charming, with a welcoming membership and beautiful property. Like many British clubs, West Sussex is best known by the name of the adjacent town, in this case, Pulborough. The course has three distinct sections. The first is elegant yet challenging without being too draconian. The par-3 sixth is one of the best and longest downhill risk-reward holes you will ever play; give the left side of the hole a wide berth. The middle third of the course is the business end, with less scenery and a strong set of par-4s. The charming closing third finishes with the slightly uphill eighteenth that's a fitting end to a really fine course.

The members are justifiably proud of their course and its low-key clubhouse. Public footpaths and bridleways crisscross the course, so don't be surprised if, suddenly, a horse gallops along while you are trying to play a shot.

THE PERFECT
EIGHTEEN HOLES

The goal of this chapter is to introduce you to some eclectic and worthy clubs, courses, and enclaves by choosing and describing eighteen magnificent holes selected from courses in North America, Scotland, Ireland, England, Northern Ireland, and Wales that would make a perfect round. For this exercise, I have chosen holes that are not part of the resorts or destinations described in the previous chapter; I have not included the seventh or eighth at Pebble Beach, the fifth at Pinehurst No. 2, or the fifth at Casa de Campo. Looking through the list, you might also ask, "What about the twelfth at Augusta?" or "Where's the sixteenth at Cypress Point?" Augusta National and Cypress Point Golf Club are private; the eighteen holes in this chapter are open to anyone. Besides, well-known holes at courses such as Augusta and Cypress are so famous that inclusion in this chapter would be superfluous; my goal is to point you in the direction of clubs and courses that are (slightly) off the beaten path. They're not quite hidden gems but not the behemoths of international golf travel, either. If there's a touch of bias toward courses in the Carolinas, I make no apologies. I live in North Carolina, and North and South Carolina are two of the top golf states in the country; there are enough great golf holes here to fill several books.

I hope you get a chance to play all eighteen of the courses in this chapter. They are well worth the effort. While I have attempted to put these in order precisely, please excuse some license with the routing.

∾ ONE ∽

THE FIRST AT THE MACHRIHANISH GOLF CLUB
CAMPBELTOWN, ARGYLL, SCOTLAND
+44.0.1586.810277
WWW.MACHGOLF.COM
428 YARDS, PAR-4

Perched on the southwest corner of the Kintyre Peninsula on Scotland's rugged and wild Atlantic coast, Machrihanish is home to the world's finest opening hole—according to Jack Nicklaus and just about everyone else. The hole perfectly combines epic scenery, natural splendor, and excellent strategic design. The tee, across the road from the warm and hospitable clubhouse, is perched some twenty to thirty feet above a wide and sandy beach. On the tee, the intelligent golfer must decide about how much of the aforementioned beach to cut off in order to find the wide fairway set at approximately forty-five degrees to the tee. The timid will fetch the fairway easily by aiming to the right but will face a long and tortuous approach to the green. The brave golfer who pulls off the more aggressive shot to the left will have a much easier second, but if the gambit fails, then the second will either find the beach (which is in play as a lateral hazard) or nestle in some of the club's infamous rough. There's risk, too, for the middling player who takes the middle route: a drive that's a hair too long will likely find one of three horrible fairway pot bunkers in the semi-rough that's shared with the eighteenth.

Many good holes are often excellent driving holes and nothing more, but the first at Machrihanish retains its quality throughout. Deep pot bunkers and penal long grass will catch anything short and wayward on the approach, and the green, set in a shallow bowl, has some wicked undulations and shelves. Wind, a factor at Machrihanish 365 days a year, adds to the appeal and challenge, as do the fast and firm conditions of the summer months. The better golfer will want an opening four, but the mid- to high-handicapper should perhaps proceed with caution and walk away happy with a sensible bogey.

The Rest of the Course

Well-known (in Scotland) as one of Scotland's top links courses, the front of this classic "out and back" routing winds through towering dunes and is the more scenic of the two nines. The back nine is the "business" side of the course, but many tees offer the best views of the Atlantic and the green and sparkling islands of Islay and Jura. Don't be shy about introducing yourself to the locals.

Getting There

By car, it's a three-hour drive from Glasgow that can be scenically beautiful in good weather but tiring in rain or fog. British Airways operates two daily flights on weekdays to nearby Campbeltown Airport, usually in a Twin Otter. The flight from Glasgow is part of the adventure. There's also an on-again, off-again ferry to Northern Ireland. The best way to enjoy Machrihanish is to spend a few days there so that you get at least one day of decent weather. It's worth the effort and not just for the first hole.

✌ TWO ✎

THE SECOND AT THE GREENBRIER RESORT
WHITE SULPHUR SPRINGS, WEST VIRGINIA
800.453.4858
WWW.GREENBRIER.COM
403 YARDS, PAR-4

It was extremely difficult for me to keep the Greenbrier out of the destinations in the previous chapter. The resort is one of America's great treasures, and its three golf courses are masterpieces of old-school mountain magic. The second hole at the Greenbrier Course is not terribly long by modern standards, but it requires just the right mix of brains and brawn. With an early morning tee time, the second, especially in the fall, is a beautiful hole, with the trees reflecting in the small lake that runs down the entire right side of the hole. The green, too, is flanked by water, and the best spot in the fairway from which to attack is probably the left center, although the fairway is slightly flatter toward the water. The green complex has two bunkers, short right and long left, and there are seemingly no easy hole locations.

The Rest of the Courses

All three courses are first-rate. The Meadows Course is probably the most scenic of the three and has the best views. The Old White is the work of two of the titans of early American golf school architecture, Charles Blair Macdonald and Seth Raynor. The massive and storied resort probably offers the most varied and complete menu of activities of any resort—anything from fly fishing to mountain biking, croquet to bowling, even serious hunting for pheasant and other game birds at the resort's private hunting preserve.

Getting There

It could not be easier. Take Interstate 64 from Beckley or Charleston, West Virginia, and look for the signs; it's exit 175 or 181. The official airport is Greenbrier Valley, which has Delta service from New York and Atlanta.

✐ THREE ✐

THE THIRD AT THE ROYAL COUNTY DOWN
(NO. 1 COURSE)
NEWCASTLE, COUNTY DOWN, NORTHERN IRELAND
+44.0.28.4372.3314
WWW.ROYALCOUNTYDOWN.ORG
477 YARDS, PAR-4

With the beautiful Mourne Mountains as an enticing backdrop and the Irish Sea within clear view, Royal County Down provides one of the finest and most stunning settings for golf. But as the third hole proves, golf at Royal County Down is not about vacation or holiday golf. It's serious stuff, and the intelligent golfer who thinks he or she has started to become good or better than decent at this game should venture to Newcastle on a windy day. Proof of its difficulty comes at the par-4 third, 477 yards from the back tees and 457 from the member's regular tees. The hole has almost twenty bunkers to provide some added spice, and some of them cross the middle of the fairway. Thus, depending on the wind, there's a decision to be made at the elevated tee; the longer hitter can carry the raised left-hand bunker, leaving a good line to the green. The second shot is no bargain, even for the big hitter, as it must be played precisely with either a fairway wood or long iron; anything that's poorly struck will bounce to the right of the fast, flattish green. A strong southerly breeze will help but might bring additional cross bunkers into play. And if you think this hole is difficult, the fourth, a 212-yard par-3 is even harder.

The Rest of the Course

Many of the holes lie between the dunes in narrow valleys, and there are plenty of blind shots, especially off the tee. Thankfully, markers show you the best general direction for the shot. Stray from the fairway, and life quickly becomes miserable in the thick grass and impenetrable gorse, so goal No. 1 must be to get the ball to the short grass. Goal No. 2 is to keep the ball out of the bunkers—there are more than 100 of varying sizes and shapes. The one redeeming feature for the modest golfer at Royal County Down is that many of the greens are open in front, so it's usually possible to bounce the ball onto the green. You could even putt it from seventy yards and in if you felt so moved.

Getting There

Royal County Down is thirty miles south of Belfast; the drive takes about one hour. It is ninety miles north of Dublin, and the drive takes about two hours. The two closest airports are about an hour by car: Belfast International Airport and Dublin Airport. Newcastle is thirty miles from the Belfast Ferry Terminals, with service to many major English and Scottish ferry ports.

৩ FOUR ৩

THE FOURTH AT BANFF SPRINGS
BANFF, ALBERTA, CANADA
866.540.4406 OR 403.762.2211
WWW.FAIRMONT.COM/BANFFSPRINGS
171 YARDS, PAR-3

You'll enjoy postcard-pretty sites at the Fairmont Banff Springs, a course that Scottish-born Canadian architect Stanley Thompson designed in 1927 in the heart of the Canadian Rockies. Thompson's nickname was "the Toronto Terror," and there must be quite a few intelligent golfers who feel slightly terrorized by the fourth at Banff, a short hole over a glacial lake. The hole is called The Devil's Cauldron, and the resort, with good reason, uses photos of the hole in its promotional efforts. From the regular tees, the hole is slightly more manageable at just 157 yards. The carry from the elevated tee must be negotiated, but the good news is that the bowl-shaped green tends to funnel shots toward the middle of the smallish putting surface. It's one of the most beautiful holes in Canadian golf.

The Rest of the Course

It's rock solid from the first hole to the last, a course with buxom beauty and the brains to match. Banff features one of the finest early examples of strategic design in North America, which led to plenty of additional work for "the Terror," not just in Canada but in the United States as well. The course plays through the magnificent forests around the main hotel and finishes with a huge par-5, 578 yards from the back tees. The resort is palatial—especially after its most recent major makeover. And you're entirely likely to encounter serious wildlife on the golf course.

Getting There

Banff Springs was originally a railroad hotel, built by the Canadian Pacific Railway. But today, most people fly to Calgary and take a shuttle or rent a car to cover the eighty-mile drive to the hotel.

ᔕ FIVE ᔕ

THE FIFTH AT LAHINCH GOLF CLUB
LAHINCH, COUNTY CLARE, IRELAND
353.0.65.7081003
WWW.LAHINCHGOLF.COM
154 YARDS, PAR-3

Those who firmly believe that blind holes should be banned from the game (and count several modern golf course architects among that number) should visit the famous "Dell" at Lahinch. Old Tom Morris came up with the idea for this hole. From the tee, all you can see are dunes and a white marker indicating the best line. Choose the right club for the distance, make a good swing, and the rest is pretty much in the hands of the golfing deities. You might get a good bounce and end up on the green, hidden deep in the dunes. Or you may receive your just deserts for too much indulgence the night before and end up in the greenside bunker. You will not find out the result of your shot until you stride up to the green. For the overall sanity of all intelligent golfers everywhere, it's probably best that the golf world includes only a few holes like this one, but as a way to make an enjoyable golf course even more interesting and fun, it's a total success at Lahinch.

The Rest of the Course

The setting seems remote, yet Lahinch is not that far from civilization. The wind and weather can howl in off the Atlantic, so be warned, but if your only visit takes place during a gale, you should still make the effort to get out of the clubhouse. The views of the Atlantic are wonderful and the turf routinely superb: Lahinch has one of the most textbook pieces of pure linksland anywhere. It's no surprise that just about every golf tour to Ireland includes this course. For those looking for luxury accommodations, head for the Lahinch Golf and Leisure Hotel. But if you've just finished your round and there's enough summer daylight available for another eighteen, go around again and enjoy this gem.

Getting There

The course is northwest of Shannon, which has summer air service from Philadelphia and flights to and from many European destinations. Galway is also close. Tipperary is in the general vicinity, but it's not that close.

⌘ SIX ⌘

THE SIXTH AT HIGHLANDS LINKS GOLF CLUB
INGONISH BEACH, NOVA SCOTIA, CANADA
800.441.1118 OR 902.285.2600
WWW.HIGHLANDSLINKSGOLF.COM
537 YARDS, PAR-5

We're back in Canada at a golf course that may be the best in this golf-crazy country. It's certainly one of the more remote locations, up on the northeastern tip of Nova Scotia on roughly the same latitude as Montreal and Quebec City. Like Banff, Highlands Links is a Stanley Thompson course routed through woods, but obviously, the surrounding topography is not as severe. Which of the par-5s is the best at Cape Breton Highlands? That's a superb question that evidently creates quite a bit of controversy among the locals who have the privilege of playing this great golf course regularly.

The sixth, ironically, is a relatively flat hole with just the elevated tee creating any movement. From the back tee, the hole requires a big tee shot into the prevailing wind and over the water hazard that flanks the left side of the hole. Golfers who have wisely chosen the forward tees will find that their angle of approach (and the length of the hole) is more reasonable. The hole offers many angles of attack, with the boldest golfers venturing closest to the water.

The Rest of the Course

Take your birdie at the sixth, if you can, as the other par-5s are big meanies, including the very next hole, a whopping 570 yards. The course starts around the shore, then heads inland over hilly but excellent golf terrain. The final holes offer shore views and are among the most beautiful on the course. The best time to play this magical course is in the fall, when the changing leaves provide one of the finest backdrops in the game.

Getting There

This is not the easiest journey in the world, but it's well worth the effort. From Sydney, where there is a small airport with flights from Halifax and Montreal, it's about eighty miles to Ingonish. From Halifax, where there is a bigger airport, it's almost 300 miles.

∽ Seven ∽

The Seventh at Pasatiempo Golf Club
Santa Cruz, California
831.459.9155
www.pasatiempo.com
346 yards, par-4

Pasatiempo, not that far from the Monterey Peninsula, is somewhat of a rarity these days: a semi-private Alister MacKenzie course that anyone with the requisite desire can play. The fourth is not the most famous hole on the course, but it's the tightest par-4—and relatively short—yet it can wreak havoc on the scorecard. Unless you are consistently laser-like off the tee, throttle back and hit a fairway wood or hybrid just to get in the fairway. The hole has a number of those stylish MacKenzie bunkers, including one that will catch the big hitter who tries to get too close to the green with an aggressive drive. The best approach is from the left side of the fairway to the long, kidney-shaped green.

The Rest of the Course

It's not long by modern standards, but Pasatiempo plays much longer than the scorecard. A number of today's top golf architects consider MacKenzie to be the finest architect. Pasatiempo clearly had a special place in his heart because he lived right next to the sixth fairway. The course has a strong membership but sets aside tee times every day for public play. Pasatiempo is highly ranked in all the golf publications, both in the overall U.S. rankings and on "places you can play" lists. And with good reason. The course is a hair tight in places due to the trees and housing that surround the course, but it has stayed true to its design roots through the years. If you are in the Monterey Peninsula area for some golf and want to see a MacKenzie gem, book a tee time and make the one-hour drive.

Getting There

Because it is tucked away somewhat, Pasatiempo recommends that you go with their directions and not rely on online map routing. It's about one hour from San Jose and ten minutes from downtown Santa Cruz.

✆ Eight ✆

The Eighth at Arcadia Bluffs Golf Club
Arcadia, Michigan
800.494.8666
WWW.ARCADIABLUFFS.COM
449 yards, par-4

From the regular tee, the hole is mercifully shorter at 389 yards and should provide a good birdie opportunity. The key is a well-struck drive that hugs the right side of the fairway and flirts (but not too much) with a bunker that's in the middle of the fairway about eighty to 100 yards from the green. This aggressive approach should leave only a short iron; the shot must avoid the deep grass-faced bunker that guards the center and right portions of the green. If you are between clubs on this hole, take the extra club and make a full swing.

The Rest of the Course

This highly regarded course in northern Michigan opened in 1999 right next to Lake Michigan. It can be windy here. The course has a links-style look and sits high above the lake, offering views that seem to go on forever. Rick Smith and his design team made excellent use of this terrific property, providing intelligent golfers with a chance to experience Scottish- and Irish-style golf in this terrific setting. In places, the course looks like the Whistling Straits courses at Kohler, only less severe and more forgiving. It offers wide fairways and large greens yet tall and nasty fescue roughs for those who stray. Just after opening, the course quickly jumped into numerous regional and national rankings.

Getting There

The nearest large town is Manistee, which has regional commercial service. Otherwise, it's more than 200 miles from Detroit or Chicago by car.

ɕ NINE ɕ

THE NINTH AT SHADOW CREEK
LAS VEGAS, NEVADA
866.260.0069
WWW.SHADOWCREEK.COM
409 YARDS, PAR-4

The best course by the most sought-after and bankable modern golf course architect, Tom Fazio, Shadow Creek opened in 1989 as the personal golf course of

Steve Wynn, the Las Vegas casino and property developer. Before the course changed hands, it was possibly the least-played golf course in the United States. That's changed now, slightly, as it's part of the MGM Mirage. At Shadow Creek, Fazio took a broad swathe of desert and turned it into the mountains of North Carolina, complete with evergreens. The ninth hole is a par-4 of modest length; there's a glorious view of the surrounding mountains from the tee. The bold intelligent golfer will take a line down the left side of the fairway, flirting with a large bunker and the stream (Shadow Creek). This will shorten the approach but bring water into play. The conservative route is to take the right side then avoid the creek on the approach. It's as solid a modern strategic hole as you'll find anywhere.

The Rest of the Course

Shadow Creek has to be seen to be believed. It's not just a golf course, it's a show. It seems almost impossible that someone could have created this type of golf course in the middle of such a bare and barren desert. From the back tees, the course is more than 7,100 yards and, like a good Vegas show, builds to a huge climax with two holes that are dramatic but could easily yield birdies. If you're a high roller at one of the MGM Mirage properties, you'll likely have the opportunity to play the course. But if you simply want to play the course, that can be arranged as well.

Getting There

Just fly or drive to Las Vegas, stay at one of the MGM Resorts International properties in Las Vegas (Bellagio, Mandalay Bay, etc.), then see what the concierge can do for you. You'll get a personal limousine ride to the course plus your own caddy for the day—if you get the nod.

∞ Ten ∞

The Tenth at Pumpkin Ridge (Ghost Creek)
North Plains, Oregon
503.647.4747
WWW.PUMPKINRIDGE.COM
492 yards, par-5

One of two wonderful golf courses at Pumpkin Ridge, Ghost Creek is perhaps the lesser known. Its back nine begins with something that every back nine should begin with, a birdie opportunity—and one that's downwind to boot. If there's a strong breeze behind you and you are feeling especially strong after that midround hot dog or snack, take on the right-hand fairway bunker. Once past that, you'll have a straight shot to the green. If you're not so bold, head left and, unless you are a massive ball striker, you'll not reach the cluster of bunkers long left. The stream that meanders through the middle of the hole should not come into play unless you hit an iron or fairway wood off the tee, in which case you'll have a decision to make—left or right of the creek. The hole, in many ways, pushes you to go for the green in two. Whether you start with a four then depends on the quality of your pitch or chip to the green.

The Rest of the Courses

The Witch Hollow Course is private but excellent. The Ghost Creek Course is solid throughout, and the front nine has some big, muscular holes that seriously tested the professionals when they played the Nike Tour Championship there in 1993 and 1994. So choose your tees carefully. The tenth may be a hair easier, and overall, the back nine is shorter and demands more finesse, especially on the wonderful seventeenth, a short par-4 just 329 yards from the back tees. Set in rural Oregon yet relatively close to civilization, the general feel of the course is pleasant and laid-back.

Getting There

The course is twenty minutes from Portland and easy to reach from Portland International Airport.

ᨒ ELEVEN ᨒ

THE ELEVENTH AT BETHPAGE BLACK
FARMINGDALE, NEW YORK
516.249.0700
WWW.NYSPARKS.STATE.NY.US/PARKS
430 YARDS, PAR-4

Of the five courses at Bethpage, the most famous is the Black, which hosted the 2002 U.S. Open. The course is the work of A.W. Tillinghast, who built a number of very difficult golf courses in the New York City area. There are no breathers at Bethpage, and the eleventh hole is proof. The hole is also visually deceptive, with a fairway that looks wider than it actually is and a green that's perched a little higher than it looks and usually requires at least one more club from the fairway. In fact, off the tee, the fairway is set at a slight angle to the right, meaning that the line with the driver is to the right of the green in the distance.

The Rest of the Course

Par at the eleventh is a great score, and the same could be said for every hole at Bethpage Black. The sign by the first tee issues this stern warning: "The Black Course is an Extremely Difficult Course Which We Recommend Only for Highly Skilled Golfers." Golfers typically sleep in their cars to get the prime tee times at Bethpage Black; for most, that means they are simply waiting in line to get their brains beaten out. Some golf course architects add a modicum of ease and playability to their designs so that average golfers can get around and enjoy themselves. That's not the case at Bethpage Black. Bailouts are few and far between, and almost every approach requires a perfectly struck iron to a heavily bunkered green that quite often looks like it's perched on the side of a cliff. It's always fun to take on a challenge, but you might want to try one of the other five courses before tackling this one—unless you're a top amateur or aspiring professional.

Getting There

The course is located east of New York City on Long Island, south of I-495.

☙ TWELVE ❧

THE TWELFTH AT WILD DUNES (LINKS COURSE)
ISLE OF PALMS, SOUTH CAROLINA
888.778.1876
WWW.WILDDUNES.COM
192 YARDS, PAR-3

If you are playing the back tees at Wild Dunes, then you'll find yourself on a rather lonely pod high above the surrounding landscape. You'll be staring at a hole that seems not to exist, due to the elevation drop. To boot, the wind is likely howling across the hole from right to left off the sea. The view is a little clearer from the regular tees, and the shot is about thirty yards easier, but it remains one of the most perilous par-3s on the South Carolina coast. The view is fine straight ahead, backward, and to the left. There's a low-rise building to the right that is not especially attractive, especially when there's a person hanging out on a balcony or walkway watching. The green is relatively small and slopes markedly away and to the right from the tee. Left is not a picnic, and right might be dead among the scrub. Long is awful, so the only place to miss might be in front of the green. Putting is tough, as well, especially if you are on the wrong side of the buried elephant in front of the green. If you choose the right club and get the shot right, you'll be putting for a birdie. If not, you could quickly pile up a big number.

The Rest of the Course

Wild Dunes is early Tom Fazio, when he was a young Turk full of vim who hadn't yet come up with a look, feel, or template. Before the housing and condos came in, the course had a raw look—and it still has plenty of that feel. It's narrow in places, wide in others, and every hole is interesting. The best holes play out to the ocean, beginning with the par-4 fifteenth.

It's pure brilliance from there all the way to the small but welcoming clubhouse. It's a special place, bold at times, quirky at others, but always a lot of fun to play, especially in a good breeze.

Getting There
The course lies about thirty minutes from downtown Charleston, South Carolina, at the northern end of the Isle of Palms.

∾ THIRTEEN ∾

THE THIRTEENTH AT NORTH BERWICK (WEST)
NORTH BERWICK, EAST LOTHIAN, SCOTLAND
01620.895040
WWW.NORTHBERWICKGOLFCLUB.COM
365 YARDS, PAR-4

We're back across the ocean this time, specifically to Scotland. Across the Firth of Forth from Fife and east of Edinburgh lies a rich vein of superb links courses, the most famous of which is Muirfield, home of the Honourable Company of Edinburgh Golfers and an Open Championship venue many times over. North Berwick is a small town with an enviable pure links course that is one of the oldest golf courses in the world. The thirteenth hole, which is an even more palatable 340 yards or so from the regular tees, is named "The Pit" because the green sits in a small hollow next to the beach. In naming certain golf holes and golf hole features, the Scots are perhaps guilty of a touch of hyperbole. There is nothing necessarily out of the ordinary in the golf world about a golf hole in a slight hollow, but the thirteenth has a stone wall that runs along the entire right side of the green. The unique obstacle denies access from the ground and requires a well-judged wedge or short iron depending on the wind, which is almost always a factor. Once you are safely aboard, however, the possibility exists for a well-deserved three.

The Rest of the Course

North Berwick is fun and even quirky. The fifteenth hole, the famous Redan, is an oft-imitated par-3. The green is set at an angle of forty-five degrees to the tee, creating thousands of permutations based on wind and hole placement. Oh, and it's about 190 yards! The first is a curious hole, as is the last, which is only about 270 yards. But that's golf in Scotland, especially early golf. Those who laid out courses in golf's early period followed the land and took what they could get from the natural features. If there were only 270 yards left for the eighteenth, then the hole was 270 yards. And there are plenty of examples of this in Scotland: the Old Course at St. Andrews is one; Prestwick Golf Club is another. Note the sign near the first hole that states, *emphatically*, "A round of golf should not take more than three hours." One reason that fast golf is possible at North Berwick is the relative paucity of deep, deep rough. Compare this to nearby Muirfield, where a poorly struck ball will submarine under the thick stuff and likely never be found again. Still, the fair burghers of North Berwick are correct. A round of golf should not take more than three hours.

Getting There

Head south then east along the A1 from Edinburgh. North Berwick is about an hour by car from the capital. Many touring golfers set up camp at the Greywalls Hotel, right next to Muirfield. From there, the group can enjoy all the wonderful courses in this corner of Scotland.

ᘒ Fourteen ᘒ

The Fourteenth at Aspen Golf Club
Aspen, Colorado
970.429.1949 or 970.925.2145
www.aspenrecreation.com
166 yards, par-3

Between downtown Aspen and the entrance to the Buttermilk Ski Resort, the Aspen Golf Club provides summer and fall fun for locals and visitors. It's a public facility that the local government runs and operates. In early April, it's often possible to ski in the morning, then play golf in the afternoon. Even though it's right in the middle of some of the most beautiful mountains in the Rockies, specifically the Elk Range, Aspen Golf Club is relatively flat and in the winter is reserved primarily for cross-country skiing. The fourteenth hole is over water, but the water should not come into play. The problem is the green that tends to repel shots not perfectly struck—sort of like a green transported from Pinehurst No. 2 and plopped down in the middle of the Roaring Fork Valley. The good news is that the altitude means more distance. The hole measures 166 yards but will play closer to 150.

The Rest of the Course

There aren't many municipal courses in the United States like Aspen Golf Club. It is not the widest golf course in the world, and the greens are not the largest. But the views are among the finest of any inland course—despite the proximity of some holes to busy Colorado Highway 82. The defining feature is a branch of the mighty Roaring Fork River, which meanders through the course and can create all sorts of havoc for the intelligent golfer who is having a bad day. Tantalizingly close, in fact right next door, is the famous Maroon Creek Golf Club, one of the most exclusive and private golf enclaves in the world. In the summer, try to get out early; afternoon thunderstorms are common.

Getting There

Take Colorado 82 northwest from Aspen about two miles from downtown. The course is on the right.

◦ꙮ Fifteen ꙮ◦

The Fifteenth at Ganton Golf Club
Ganton, North Yorkshire, England
+44.0.1944.710329
www.gantongolfclub.com
465 yards, par-4

From the first hole to somewhere near the twelfth, Ganton seems and plays like a relatively straightforward golf course—with some superb holes to be sure. But from the thirteenth to before the obvious delineation of the eighteenth, things get murky at Ganton, even on a clear summer's day. The holes lose their definition, and the golf course assumes the look of the African veldt, albeit dotted with bunkers and surprising quantities of gorse. In the middle of this golfing muddle, or riddle, is a beast of a par-4, the fifteenth. The hole plays slightly uphill and into a southerly breeze. The course has a difficult, oddly shaped bunker that must be avoided at all costs even though the fairway is very wide; big hitters might even have to throttle back to avoid this semi-chasm. The second shot is long and tortuous, and a par will almost always win the hole.

The Rest of the Course

Yorkshire is a cricket-mad county, with golf a bit of an afterthought, so Ganton is an oasis for the serious intelligent golfer. Gentlemen must wear a jacket and tie at all times in the clubhouse of this highly traditional course. Somewhere near the dawn of civilization, Ganton was near the coast, and it's still possible to find seashells in some of the bunkers even though the course is now several miles from the sea. Oh, those bunkers! They are some of the deepest of any golf course in England, often several feet below the level of the green. There aren't any jaw-dropping golf holes on this flattish piece of property in the Vale of Mowbray, but each is solid in its own way. The course is definitely worth a visit if you are in the north of England; it's open to some public play, but be sure to call well ahead. Also of note: the course has hosted the Ryder Cup, the Walker Cup, and the Curtis Cup, three of the major team golf events.

Getting There

From York, take the A64 east to Scarborough. The course is on the left about eleven miles before Scarborough.

❧ SIXTEEN ❧

THE SIXTEENTH AT PINE NEEDLES
SOUTHERN PINES, NORTH CAROLINA
910.692.7111
WWW.PINENEEDLES-MIDPINES.COM
180 YARDS, PAR-3

At first glance, and from a purely aesthetic standpoint, the sixteenth hole is clearly the inferior of the four excellent par-3s at Pine Needles, the wonderfully relaxed Donald Ross course just a few miles from Pinehurst Resort and Country Club. The par-3 third is the most photographed. The par-3 fifth is the hardest, and the par-3 thirteenth is the most perplexing, especially when the hole is cut toward the back of the green. So what is it about the sixteenth that warrants any attention? Of the four short holes at Pine Needles, it's the one that requires and rewards the best shot. The hole is relatively flat, if a little uphill, so the target landing area is not always obvious, which often makes club selection difficult. A thin shot that's short is acceptable unless the hole is in the back portion of the green; in this instance, the subtle undulations and burrows on the green make getting up and down a difficult task. The four-foot cliff at the back of the green also makes life interesting. Anything right or left will find deep bunkers that only a skilled bunker player will find amusing. It's not the most famous hole at Pine Needles, which held the U.S. Women's Open for the third time in 2007, and not the most popular, but the sixteenth is easily the most underrated.

The Rest of the Course

One of the finest courses in the Pinehurst/Southern Pines Area, Pine Needles has hosted the U.S. Women's Open three times. A recent makeover using pre-war photos restored the course to its original state, or at least close to it. Few courses provide such total consistency from the first hole to the eighteenth: every hole is strong yet completely playable for the average golfer. The par-3s are excellent and perhaps one of the finest sets of short holes in North Carolina. But the real beef of the course comes from its par-4s, each of which provides unique challenges. The long second hole plays downhill to a green that slopes away from the fairway. The best par-4s seem to come in pairs: six and seven; eight and nine; eleven and twelve; seventeen and eighteen.

Most of the greens at Pine Needles feature some steep slopes to the side and back, thus causing the large greens to play much smaller. Charming, fun, walkable, entertaining, and storied, Pine Needles is what intelligent golf is all about.

Getting There

Pine Needles is located on Midland Road near the intersection with U.S. 1. From U.S. 1, take the Midland Road exit. From the traffic circle, follow signs to Southern Pines; Pine Needles will be on your left.

⊘ Seventeen ⊘

The Seventeenth at the Tournament Players
Club Sawgrass (Stadium Course)
Ponte Vedra Beach, Florida
904.273.3235
www.tpc.com/sawgrass
140 yards, par-3

Normally, a touring golf professional would look at a 140-yard hole and think instantly about a birdie. At the seventeenth at the original Tournament Players Club, the pros are thinking about bogeys or worse— or at least about *avoiding* them. It's this type of mind inversion that Stadium Course architect Pete Dye wants when connecting with the professionals. The green is, for all intents and purposes, an island, albeit with a narrow isthmus. There is no bailout. You either hit and hold the small green or you are in the water, heading for the drop zone and hoping for a five. Actually, as if the hole weren't cruel enough, Dye comically put a small pot bunker in front of the green. Oh—and the wind can swirl here, making club selection even more difficult. The hole usually ranks as one of the hardest during The Players Championship, held each year at Sawgrass.

The Rest of the Course

The Stadium Course offers an extremely modern golf course design. And it's an extremely difficult course from the back tees. The par-5s are excellent, especially the sixteenth. There's water, bunkers large and small, holes wide and narrow, flattish greens and wildly undulating greens. Golf at the Stadium Course is a roller coaster ride—golf schizophrenia.

Getting There

Ponte Vedra Beach is south of Jacksonville, Florida. From Jacksonville Beach, take I-95 south to the Ponte Vedra Beach exit.

⮜ EIGHTEEN ⮞

THE EIGHTEENTH AT THE HONOURABLE COMPANY
OF EDINBURGH GOLFERS
DULLANE, EAST LOTHIAN, SCOTLAND
+44.0.1620.842123
WWW.MUIRFIELD.ORG.UK
448 YARDS, PAR-4

We started in Scotland, so we'll end in Scotland at a wonderful closing hole that leads up to Muirfield's low-key clubhouse. The hole is a daunting prospect at any time of the year but especially so on the final hole of the Open Championship. The hole is narrow and well bunkered, and the green, given some sensible hole locations, can yield a birdie if you find the correct side of the ridge. But it's a long hole, even for a professional, and a par to win a championship is gratefully taken.

The Rest of the Course

Muirfield is somewhat unique among links courses in that it's not an out-and-back routing but more like two loops, one inside the other, one going counter-clockwise, the other running clockwise. This makes gauging the wind a tough proposition from hole to hole. The first and most important job at Muirfield is staying out of the deep, nasty, horrid rough. It's a shot penalty, in essence—assuming you can even find the ball. One of the most historic golf clubs in the world, Muirfield is also one of the most formal—and revered. Its scant "public" tee times are like gold dust in summer, and visitors are expected to behave in accordance with the traditions of the club, including wearing a jacket and tie inside. Most groups that visit stay for the day, playing a four-ball in the morning, then a foursome (alternate shot) in the afternoon. The afternoon round should perhaps be seen as less serious than the morning round, for the lunch at Muirfield is excellent and includes numerous Scottish specialties that require quite a bit of washing down.

Getting There

The route is essentially the same as for North Berwick. The Greywalls Hotel is immediately adjacent to the eighteenth hole at Muirfield.

3

NINE HIDDEN GEMS

The golf destinations in this chapter are not necessarily off the beaten path, and some aren't really all that hidden anymore. But the destinations here are often overlooked, especially by golfers who know little about resorts outside their region. A golfer in North Carolina knows all too well about the quality of Pine Needles and Mid Pines and knows all about Pebble Beach, but a golfer in California probably knows very little about Pine Needles and Mid Pines.

The selections here are not the behemoths of the golf resorts but places where the golf is often just as good and the setting more regional and even, dare I say it, a touch more intimate. The big, historic, world-renowned resorts are fun, and each is wonderful and epic in its own way. But the hidden gems, while lacking certain amenities and fame, are often perfect spots for those who are looking for golf in a more relaxed and low-key setting.

⊰⊱ One ⊰⊱

Pine Needles Lodge & Golf Club
Mid Pines Inn & Golf Club
Southern Pines, North Carolina
910.692.7111 or 910.692.2114
www.pineneedles-midpines.com

Built in the 1920s, Mid Pines and Pine Needles are first cousins and, in fact, reside right across the road from each other about five miles from Pinehurst Resort. Mid Pines has had different owners over the years, but Pine Needles has had the same owners—the Bell family—for several decades. When, about ten years ago, the matriarch of the Bells, Peggy Kirk Bell, had the opportunity to purchase Mid Pines, she jumped at the chance. So now Mid Pines and Pine Needles are actually related, and you can enjoy both as part of a package.

Both locations have wonderful Donald Ross courses that the great golf course architect personally supervised. They are different courses in many ways, and their adjuncts differ, but they offer the same level and quality of golf and relaxation throughout. Both have wonderful settings for the game, and the service is more familial than corporate. As soon as you set foot on either property, you feel like you are in someone's home—and for all intents and purposes, you are!

After a successful restoration, Pine Needles is a charming course that has now hosted the U.S. Women's Open three times. Thankfully, when you play the course, it will not be set up like it was for these events: the rough will not be as long, the bunkers not as steep, and hole locations not so demonic. As a result, Pine Needles is a course that every intelligent golfer can enjoy. It has many of the Ross features often found in the area, including strategically placed fairway bunkers and steep slopes at the edges of some greens. But the angles are not so severe at Pine Needles and the test not as tortuous as the one found just up Midland Road at Pinehurst No. 2. The better golfer will feel that par is attainable on just about every hole, while the average golfer will not card a lot of really big numbers. That's true until the par-5 fifteenth, where the course finally bears some serious teeth. The eighteenth hole, tumbling down to the narrow green, is one of the best closers in North Carolina.

While Pine Needles is the predictable and well-mannered daughter who finishes high school with good grades and graduates from college on time, Mid Pines is the wild child, the unpredictable and moody cousin who would do anything at any time. Narrower, quirkier, and tougher on and around the greens, Mid Pines is the course where a good golfer looks at the card and thinks that it will be a relatively easy morning yet often leaves with a black eye and bruised ego. That's because Mid Pines has some difficult, difficult holes where it's easy to get out of position. The par-3 second is a mid-iron to a green that seems to want to repel anything and everything. The par-4 fourth is almost comically short, but the back section of the green is minute and anything right of the green will trickle annoyingly down a blind cliff toward some condos. And the next hole, a short-ish par-5, has a pond placed in the most annoying spot possible. This goes on until you finally helicopter a club into a loblolly pine. There are places around the greens where even Dave Pelz, the short-game wizard, would feel totally bamboozled.

The accommodations are different but stately and old-fashioned. Mid Pines has a beautiful hotel that provides the backdrop for the fine eighteenth hole. The floorboards squeak and bend, but that's part of the price of admission. Pine Needles has more of a lodge feel, with many of the rooms overlooking the practice area and first hole. Mid Pines has a fine restaurant, where you will need a jacket and tie. Pine Needles is less formal, and the lunchtime buffet featuring the best of serious Southern cooking is not to be missed; also check out the unique sunken bar. Whereas the range at Mid Pines is middling at best, the practice facilities at Pine Needles are among the most extensive in the United States. The excellent school hosts "Golfaris," multiday schools perfect for the intelligent golfer aspiring to better days.

You could spend more than a month exploring all the wonderful golf in and around the Pinehurst area, but at the end of the month, you'll probably remember Mid Pines and Pine Needles as the most relaxed and traditional environment for the game in the entire region. The moment you walk into Pine Needles or Mid Pines, you will feel right at home. And you will *always* feel that way.

◦ TWO ◦

Bay Hill Club & Lodge
Orlando, Florida
888.422.9445
www.bayhill.com

There's not exactly a paucity of golf resorts in central Florida, and each has to work hard to separate itself from the crowd. Bay Hill maintains its stature through its association with Arnold Palmer and its yearly appearance on the PGA Tour. So calling Bay Hill "hidden" is totally inaccurate. But calling it a "gem" is precisely correct.

Located southwest of downtown Orlando, Bay Hill has one course and a seventy-room lodge where nonmembers can stay and enjoy the use of the club's ample facilities. So it's more of a club where members have overnight guests than a resort—which is part of its charm. Bay Hill is very much Arnold Palmer's home, and there's a strong chance you will run into "the King" either on the golf course or enjoying a meal in the clubhouse. But be warned, the great man is keen that people not wear hats inside—especially male golfers. At the right time (not in the middle of his main course), it's entirely appropriate to introduce yourself, but the intelligent golfer understands that begging for an autograph would not be sensible.

The golf course, which Palmer designed, is serious stuff and, in many ways, mirrors Palmer's charging go-for-broke style that he employed so well when he was at the top of his game. The eighteenth is the most famous hole at Bay Hill, but the hole that most closely exemplifies the Bay Hill style is the par-5 sixth, which curves around a lake, endlessly tempting the big hitter. Or maybe it's the par-3 seventeenth, a massive 219-yard hole almost entirely over water to an exposed green.

Orlando is an energetic and curious city seemingly set in the middle of swamplands. It's a world destination but also a winter home for many who are there to relax. The city has some garishness, some neon, and some flash and sizzle. It also has some very private enclaves that few get to visit. Bay Hill is one of these, but it happens to have a sumptuous lodge for those of us who relish the thought of being a member of such an enclave for a few days.

❧ THREE ❧

THE GLENEAGLES HOTEL
AUCHTERARDER, PERTHSHIRE, SCOTLAND
0800 389 3737 (UK) OR 866.881.9525 (USA)
WWW.GLENEAGLES.COM

In Scotland, Gleneagles is hardly a hidden gem. It's one of the country's largest and most famous hotels. Yet far too many golfers from North America who visit Scotland bypass Gleneagles in their frantic rush to discover all things coastal and linksy. In a time-constrained visit, missing Gleneagles is understandable, but if you have some time, a two- or three-day respite there is almost mandatory, especially if you want a taste of Scotland's highlands, or at least its uplands. If you're looking for the perfect place to recover from jet lag, look no further than Gleneagles.

The hotel is a former country estate set on 850 acres and looks more like a French château than a Scottish nobleman's home. It opened in the 1920s and has a storied history. It's one of the largest hotels in Scotland, with 232 well-appointed rooms that, stylistically, are relatively modern. The Automobile Association, sort of the equivalent to AAA in North America, has awarded Gleneagles the highest possible rating, five red stars.

Although it's called a hotel, Gleneagles is essentially a resort but with a country sports twist. Hunting, called *shooting* in the United Kingdom, is a sport here, as are falconry and gundog training. You can also enjoy off-road driving, fly fishing, and numerous other activities, including simply lounging around in the spa.

The golf at Gleneagles is exceptional. There are three courses: the King's, the Queen's, and the PGA Centenary Course that will host the Ryder Cup in 2014. Jack Nicklaus designed the latter. The King's Course dates to 1919 and is a fine example of excellent design from "the Golden Age" of golf course architecture. The Queen's Course is a charming course and a wonderful walk through woodlands and moor. It's not links golf but moorland golf on uplands with sweeping views of the surrounding countryside—in this case the beginning of the highlands. On a clear day, the views are superb.

Those who love to eat game will be in heaven at Gleneagles, where the menu of the flagship restaurant features pigeon, duck, and venison. If you're a first-time visitor to Gleneagles, you have to try haggis, which is essentially sheep's innards cooked for about three hours in a sheep's stomach then inserted into a casing. Think of the best sausage you have ever had and then square it, and you have haggis. If it's not to your liking, the wine cellar at Gleneagles will make up for any shortcomings. The hotel has no fewer than seven sommeliers.

If you want a taste of the highlands of Scotland but in a luxurious setting, Gleneagles is your place. It's also an excellent choice for the intelligent golfer who enjoys hunting and fishing as much as golf. But if you want to hunt—sorry, shoot—grouse and other upland game birds, remember that the season begins in mid-August, the "Glorious Twelfth" to be precise; it's the beginning of September for pheasant. If you have hunted quail, duck, and even pheasant in North America, you owe it to yourself, at least once in your lifetime, to experience driven grouse shooting. It's almost as good as golf.

ເ◌ Four ◌ວ

Keystone Resort
Keystone, Colorado
877.753.9786 or 970.496.4500
www.keystoneresort.com

When you think Keystone, you likely think about snow—specifically the ski resort near the Continental Divide. In the winter, Keystone is one of Colorado's top skiing destinations. But once the snow has melted away and the mud of postseason has turned into beautiful grassy and wooded valleys (usually around mid-June), Keystone becomes a different sort of playground. One of the best places in the

Rockies to access and enjoy this playground is the Keystone Lodge and Spa.

The ski destinations in this part of Colorado are slightly higher than other locations, and the two golf courses affiliated with Keystone Lodge are up around 9,000 feet. This is great news for shorter hitters since the ball will travel significantly farther. Lodge guests have access to two courses, Keystone Ranch and the River Course at Keystone.

Keystone Ranch is routed through what used to be a ranch and lettuce farm and thus has a wider aspect than many mountain courses; think of it as a high meadow course with native sagebrush bordering many of the holes. The ranch houses the clubhouse and a restaurant that serves meals with a Western theme. The River Course has more elevation changes; wetlands, the Snake River, and even mountain biking paths are the hazards. On the back nine, the course gains even more elevation and offers excellent views of Gore Range and the Continental Divide. The sixteenth, a 509-yard par-4, features a 200-foot drop from tee to fairway. On either course, it's likely that you'll encounter wildlife at any time.

Aside from the remarkable golf, Keystone Lodge offers a wide range of outdoor-based activities, from mountain biking to hiking to yoga, and you can even take chairlift rides up to the top of the Keystone ski area. Accommodations at the property provide a pleasant combination of rusticity and comfort; the best of the 152 rooms and suites are the loft suites, which feature a living room downstairs and a plush bedroom upstairs via a spiral staircase. Keystone Lodge is at its busiest deep into ski season, but it's wonderful in the summer, and the two golf courses should whet the appetite of any golfer.

✂ FIVE ↝

GARLAND LODGE & RESORT
LEWISTON, MICHIGAN
877.442.7526
WWW.GARLANDUSA.COM

Located in the heart of Michigan's Lower Peninsula in Lewiston, Garland describes itself as "Michigan's Most Beautiful Resort." It's tough to argue with the tag line. Its beautiful woodlands are replete with streams, pines, and lakes, the setting is pristine, and there's more than enough space—approximately 3,500 acres—to help you feel like you are totally away from it all.

All four courses start from the golf shop, and each is unique enough to provide a golf group with more than enough variety over a four-day, five-night trip. The Fountains Course, which opened in 1995, has a rare combination of holes—six par-5s, six par-4s, and six par-3s—and nine of the holes have water. The

Swampfire is a more serious affair, with water on all but four holes, most of which require your full attention from tee to green. The Reflections is one of the favorites at Garland, perhaps because it's the shortest and most picturesque of the four. But it still boasts some long and muscular holes, including the par-5 fifth that's 555 yards from the back tees.

The Monarch Course is one of Michigan's longest golf courses at almost 7,200 yards; ironically, it's one of the best for women because the forward tees are set well forward at 4,904 yards. Bald eagles nest near the eleventh hole. The course has its own version of Augusta National's "Amen Corner," beginning with a 581-yard par-5 after the turn. For classic and enjoyable Michigan resort golf, it's almost impossible to beat Garland, and there aren't many resorts with four or more courses in the Midwest.

Garland is a year-round resort with plenty to keep everyone busy in winter when the courses are usually under snow. Hildegard's Dining Room is the main restaurant at Garland, although Herman's Grill offers the same menu, is less formal, and has late-night options. The menu at Hildegard's includes a broad selection of locally caught fresh fish. Accommodations at Garland vary from log cabins to golf cottages. The resort has its own airport for private planes; otherwise, it's an hour-and-a-half trip from either Traverse City Airport or Alpena Airport. If there's one reason that people make the effort to get to Garland, it's the tranquility and sheer beauty of the four golf courses, which are also very well-maintained.

Six

Eseeola Lodge
Linville, North Carolina
800.742.6717
www.eseeola.com

Eseeola Lodge is a quaint and small inn with just twenty-four rooms and suites in Linville, which is primarily a second-home retreat for families from Charlotte, Greensboro, and Winston-Salem. Linville is in the Blue Ridge Mountains near Boone in the northeastern part of North Carolina's mountains. Guests at Eseeola can access the exclusive Linville Golf Club, an early and relatively unmolested Donald Ross design that serious fly fishermen will absolutely hate: rainbow trout the size of sharks swim freely in the many streams that crisscross this wonderfully peaceful layout. Sadly, fishing is strictly forbidden at Linville, as is walking—more on that later.

For those seeking an alternative to the larger resorts—a fine bed and breakfast with an exquisite golf course—the Eseeola Lodge is the perfect fit. And unlike a typical bed and breakfast in the mountains, the Eseeola has a fine restaurant; Pan-seared Rainbow Trout in a Citrus Butter Sauce is a staple on the menu. The rooms are elegant and comfortable, and you could easily spend an entire day relaxing right there without heading to one of the common areas.

Linville Golf Club is near the site of the very first golf course in North Carolina, and the course has the look and feel of a museum piece. Donald Ross built it in 1924 and clearly left the land mostly intact, simply building tees and green sites in logical spots along the valley floor. One result of his approach is the par-4 third hole, 472 yards and one of the best that Ross ever designed. In fact, it's one of the best holes in the United States. It plays downhill to a sloping fairway then uphill to a green set on a small knoll. It's an excellent example of letting the land lead the architect. The fairways are bentgrass, but the greens are *Poa annua*, and any putt above the hole can be nightmarish. Another piece of advice: don't fly the greens. Getting up and down from behind one of the putting surfaces is pretty much impossible. Linville would be a great golf course to walk, but the club, at least in the past, has not been especially walker-friendly.

Many who visit the Eseeola Lodge are weekenders up from the "plains" to escape the summer heat. But the golf at Linville is easily good enough to warrant a longer stay. Late September and October are also excellent times to visit Eseeola.

৩ Seven ৩

Silverado Resort
Napa, California
800.532.0500
www.silveradoresort.com

For those who think that a perfect vacation or weekend break would include golf and the wonderful wines of the Napa Valley, Silverado is an excellent location. The resort sits on 1,200 acres, and its main building looks like a winemaker's retreat tucked in the valley between the attractive hills. The one-bedroom Fireplace Suite is the way to go at Silverado; it's the perfect place to congregate before heading to dinner with friends in one of the resort's three eateries, all of which offer excellent food prepared mostly with local produce and meats. And of course, your wine list will be replete with locally produced wines.

The two Robert Trent Jones Jr. courses provide an excellent complement to the resort and spa. The longer North Course is perhaps the more forgiving of the two courses, but the shorter South Course is a lot of fun as well. Both offer a taste of the beautiful Napa Valley scenery. Napa is a popular spot with tourists and visitors from all over the world who come for tours of the vineyards and wineries—the local château, if you will. Why not combine it with some golf?

◌ EIGHT ◌

BARTON CREEK RESORT & SPA
AUSTIN, TEXAS
866.572.7369 OR 512.329.4000
WWW.BARTONCREEK.COM

A Dallas-based golf teacher once told me that there weren't many good golf courses in Texas due to the topography. For the most part, he is right—until you get into Texas Hill Country around Austin. Here, the land has much more undulation, and golf course architects have more latitude to build interesting golf holes. One of the best ways to enjoy the remarkable golf in this area is at Barton Creek Resort and Spa, a AAA Four-Diamond property set on 4,000 acres of secluded property west of downtown Austin. The resort has 300 rooms, each with a view of the surrounding hills. There's also an impressive spa, four eateries on-site, and a children's program.

Once you've had enough fun at Barton Creek's miniature golf course, you'll want to head to the real thing. There are four courses at Barton Creek, plus the Chuck Cook Golf Academy. There are two Tom Fazio courses, the Fazio Foothills and the Fazio Canyons. The Arnold Palmer Lakeside course has excellent views of Lake Travis. And one of the first collaborations between Bill Coore and Ben Crenshaw is here— the Crenshaw Cliffside Course.

Most intelligent golfers in Texas are used to flattish courses with small ponds and lakes and low trees. At Barton Creek, the land has a rugged tinge for sure, but the undulations and the hazards make for serious golf often requiring heroic shots—at times, you are just going to have to hit a shot with virtually no bailout, usually over a yawning chasm. It's heaven or hell golf. Miss the shot and you'll be reaching into your pocket for a new ball, but make the shot and you'll be talking about it over dinner. Thus golf at Barton Creek is some of the most exciting and heart-pounding you will experience. Especially in Texas.

In the evenings, you can try one of the fine restaurants on-site or go downtown for the one thing that has made Austin so famous: live music.

∽ Nine ∾

BALLANTYNE HOTEL & LODGE
CHARLOTTE, NORTH CAROLINA
888.627.8048 OR 704.248.4000
WWW.BALLANTYNERESORT.COM

Opened in 2001, Ballantyne Resort is a relative newcomer compared to some of the other hidden gems in this chapter. However, the resort has already garnered some remarkable accolades and awards, including Mobil Four-Star status. Even its spa has been highly ranked by *Conde Nast Johansens*. The golf course, which opened before the main resort hotel, was named the "Best New Golf Course in North Carolina" by *North Carolina Magazine*. Ballantyne Resort also boasts the Dana Rader Golf School (top twenty-five in the United States), the lodge, the main resort hotel, the Gallery Restaurant, and tennis. The rooms are well-appointed, but it's the sumptuous bathrooms that guests enjoy the most: each room includes a massive tub that's perfect for a long soak.

Much of the weekday business is corporate oriented, but on weekends the resort is a wonderful getaway. Getting to the resort is remarkably easy; it's just fifteen minutes from Charlotte/Douglas International Airport, which has more than 500 flights a day. If you don't want to travel to some of the difficult-to-get-to resorts but still want resort-style relaxation and excellent golf and golf instruction, Ballantyne Resort is a great choice.

The nine hidden gems in this chapter represent just a sampling of the smaller, wonderful, and usually less-talked-about golf destinations. Part of the enjoyment of the game comes from exploration and discovery. While it's certainly tempting to find a favorite course and make it a regular destination, every golfer should make an effort to visit a new spot at least once every two years. My hope is that this chapter inspires you to find new places and meet new golfers.

4

PLANNING THE ULTIMATE GOLF ADVENTURE

I f you are going to visit a golf resort in North America, then booking your golf trip will be as simple as calling a toll-free number or clicking a mouse a few times. However, and especially if you are going with a group of more than two, there's a lot you can do to maximize your enjoyment of your golf trip before you contact the resort—and there's even more that you can organize after you finalize your booking.

Going overseas is an entirely different proposition, especially if one of your target destinations is Scotland or Ireland. In this instance, it's impossible to call a toll-free number and simply make all the reservations. The intelligent golfer who has his or her heart set on an adventure to the United Kingdom has two ways to go. One, organize the trip yourself, writing to the clubs you want to play, calling the hotels, and booking flights, transfers, cars, etc. Lots of people go this route, and yes, it takes considerable time. I organized a trip to England and Scotland this way, and it turned out very well—though it was for only two people. Second, you can rely on a professional golf tour specialist to organize everything for you so that your main responsibility is arriving at the airport on time on the day of departure. Either way, the checklists that follow should be helpful. Later in this chapter, you'll find advice about how to choose a tour operator.

While a spur-of-the-moment trip is always fun, the general rule of thumb is that the further ahead you plan, the more likely you are to enjoy your trip. If calling up a resort or going on the Internet isn't your bag, your travel agent can help you make all the necessary arrangements; even in this world of online booking, the most intelligent way to start a vacation is with the help of a travel specialist.

BEFORE YOU BOOK

1. Determine your group composition. Number of golfers? All men? All women? Spouses? Children?

2. Decide on your time window. Visit southern-tier resorts in the winter and northern-tier resorts in the summer. For most of California, you can go pretty much anytime. Ditto Hawaii. Visit Scotland, Ireland, England, or Wales from May through October.

3. Are you traveling during prime time or shoulder season (the period just before or after prime season)?

4. Unless there's one destination you really want to visit, and only one, narrow your choices to a short list; then have your friends over for a drink one evening to see what everyone thinks.

5. Though resort Web sites are notoriously full of mostly useless information, something the British call *bumf*, scan the Web sites and request all the brochures.

6. Ask the PGA professional at your club for his opinion. Ask the LPGA professional at your club, too, if you have one. They have probably been to some of the resorts you are considering.

7. Decide whether you want to include some instructional sessions if the resort has a well-known golf academy or school.

8. Think about how long you want to stay and whether you want to take in additional destinations or attractions.

9. If the resort has more courses than you have days of vacation, decide which courses you want to include.

10. Consider which of the resort's accommodations meet your needs.

11. If you have nongolfers in your group, look at which of the resort's nongolf activities will appeal to them.

12. Book your flights well ahead of time—especially if you are going to an area with only a small or regional airport.

13. Determine your exact itinerary—but have some flexibility.

If you book your trip armed with all the information above, you will be significantly ahead of the curve, and the chances of enjoying your trip skyrocket.

AFTER YOU BOOK

Now that you have booked your excursion, it's time to get prepared. The resort or tour specialist may have a checklist—ask for one. But here's a general checklist to keep handy:

1. Purchase a hard case for your golf bag. Many soft cases offer good protection, but some airlines require a hard case before they guarantee that your clubs will arrive with shafts and heads intact. If you have watched baggage handlers load clubs onto a plane, you'll notice that some bags fall off the conveyor belt onto the concrete. If your clubs are in a soft case and they fall fifteen feet, something is going to break.

2. Check your waterproof gear. Today's best gear is lightweight, breathable, functional, and totally waterproof. It's a vital investment.

3. Buy a pair or two of FootJoy wet gloves. These help you grip the club even when the weather is extremely wet.

4. Seriously consider trip cancellation insurance.

5. Change your grips. If it's raining, the last thing you need are worn grips.

6. Take a series of lessons (short game and long game), practice, and get your game in shape.

7. If you will be walking, purchase a bag designed specifically for walking—if you don't already have one.

8. Get in shape for the trip—especially if you are going to a walking-only resort and you don't walk that much. If you are not a fitness type or you have trouble making time to get in shape, hire a personal trainer and make weekly appointments for the six to eight weeks before your trip.

9. Visit the golf store to get balls and all other requisite accessories.

10. Make sure the nongolfers have all their activities organized.

11. Research the resort you are visiting, especially if it's an older one. If you know something about its history, you will enjoy the trip even more.

12. If you are going overseas, get all your documents in order.

Choosing a Golf Tour Specialist

If you are considering a trip to the United Kingdom or even farther afield, the first person you should ask for a referral is the golf professional at your club. Also ask friends at your club or at work. If nothing else, search online for a golf tour operator in your area—it is better to work with someone local to you, but it's not mandatory. Some groups choose to work with tour specialists in Scotland or Ireland; this has its benefits. The list of questions that follow should help you evaluate the golf tour specialists you are considering:

1. How many years have the specialists been in business?

2. Do they offer package tours or custom tours, or both?

LEARNING TO SPEAK SCOTTISH

*I*f you are going to Scotland, you might encounter a bit of a language barrier. While basic pronunciation is sometimes to blame, the root cause of the occasional misunderstanding is usually grounded in semantics. Here are some basic phrases and words that might help:

PURE: *Poor.* Caddy example: "The shot you hit, sir, was very *pure*. It's out of bounds."

AFF: *Off.* Caddy example: "Your putt was way *aff* line."

J. ARTHUR: *Shank.* This is rhyming slang: J. Arthur Rank rhymes with shank. Rank was a well-known industrialist and millionaire film producer from the London area. Caddy example: "Right on the hosel, sir, a cold *J. Arthur*."

CANNAE: *Cannot.* Caddy example: "I *cannae* tell if you're from New York or Atlanta. It's all the same to me."

CHUFFED: *Happy, delighted.* Caddy example: "You should be totally *chuffed* with that hole-in-one, sir. I would be."

SWALLY: *Alcoholic beverages.* Caddy example: "I'm a bit tired this morning, sir. I had my fair share of the *swally* last night. About forty pints."

3. Can they supply local references?

4. If they offer itineraries including St. Andrews, do they guarantee your tee time on the Old Course?

5. How are they compensated?

6. How good will they be at accommodating and organizing activities for nongolfers?

7. Will you deal directly with the owner of the firm?

8. If they are located in the United States, do they have someone "on the ground" in Scotland or Ireland?

Working with a golf tour specialist is a team effort. Once you have chosen a specialist, you'll get the best results if you stick to your itinerary and don't change it. Since clubs, hotels, and others require deposits, your tour operator will require a significant portion of the trip's cost well ahead of time—up to a year, perhaps. Keep in mind that he who tries to tell the specialist how to do his job is almost always doomed to failure. Once you have chosen your specialist, enjoy the relationship and let him do what he does best.

5

THE INFORMED GOLFER

Periodically, or perhaps a touch more often, golf can seem a bit mysterious—even to the intelligent golfer. The game has its own language and nuances, and its own way of going about its business that, especially to the relative newcomer, can seem a hair perplexing. But it's not only nascent golfers who find certain aspects of the game perplexing; every so often, a professional golfer who has been playing all day every day for decades will make a rules-related or etiquette-related blunder that will momentarily stun the golfing world, or at least the assembled media gaggle. The primary goal of this chapter is to offer some basic sagacity so that the intelligent golfer feels even more at home with the game.

Of course, the only true way to get to know golf is to play, and it would totally delight me if you were to put down this book right now and drive straight to the golf course. We should all be playing at least twice the number of rounds we currently play.

LEARNING THE GAME

Learn the Basic Rules

Even though the bodies that regulate golf have tried to simplify the rules over the past decade or so, the rules of golf can be difficult to learn and even more difficult to understand and interpret. Every intelligent golfer, however, should know the basic rules. When you join the U.S. Golf Association, which you should, the association will send you a bag tag, a towel or hat, and a copy of the rules. If, after reading this slim volume, you are confused, don't worry; you are not alone. You might wish to purchase a rules video or one of the many books that aim to clarify the rules; even top professional golfers make rules-related mistakes from time to time.

The most basic and most important rule is to play the ball as it lies, regardless of the quality of the lie. Some golfers at some clubs believe that they can move the ball around in the fairway to gain a better lie. This is cheating.

Most of all, every intelligent golfer knows that the most important unwritten rule of the game is this: enjoy yourself.

ஃ Understand and Work on ஃ the Fundamentals

The informed intelligent golfer takes regular lessons from a qualified PGA or LPGA golf teacher. Tiger Woods spends a lot of time working on his fundamentals, and so should every golfer. He works on:

- ✦ Grip
- ✦ Posture
- ✦ Ball position

- ✦ Stance
- ✦ Alignment

If all of the above are correct, your chances of hitting playable shots skyrocket. If your fundamentals are poor, you cannot be consistent—and consistency is the hallmark of every intelligent golfer.

If in Doubt, Ask

If you are a newcomer to the game and you are playing with someone who has been playing for what might seem like several decades, there is absolutely nothing wrong with saying, "I'm still relatively new to the game. I have a question about this rule or some basic etiquette." From this point on, your playing partner will be delighted to help you. Listen to what your partner has to say.

HOW TO CHOOSE A GOLF TEACHER

Do you know a golfer who has improved significantly? Let's say someone who has gone from a 17 handicap to a 7? Ask that person about his or her teacher. That lesson tee should be your first stop. The intelligent golfer knows that good teachers come in all shapes and sizes—and might be male or female. Here are some ways to recognize a good teacher when you find one:

✦ A good teacher asks you about your expectations and makes sure they are realistic.

✦ A good teacher teaches a lot and is in demand.

✦ A good teacher stresses the fundamentals and does not hesitate to fix your grip if it needs to be fixed.

✦ A good teacher emphasizes the short game as the fastest way to lower your score.

✦ A good teacher is very likely a member of the PGA or LPGA.

✦ A good teacher keeps it simple and does not bombard you with information.

If in doubt, ask around. Once you have found your teacher, the best way to make the most of your investment is to do what your teacher tells you to do; the mistake many golfers make is to let their egos get in the way. The intelligent student of golf never does. Be patient and stick with your teacher's methodology. Ignore advice from others and ignore all the advice in the golf magazines and on The Golf Channel—unless *your* teacher is in one of the golf magazines or is on The Golf Channel.

BUYING CLUBS

Every club in your golf bag should be fitted to your swing, your dimensions, and the current state of your game. Clubs bought "off the rack" from a store might work well for you, but for the best results, everything should be precisely fitted by your club professional, a stand-alone clubfitter, or an expert in a stand-alone golf store. Every club can be customized. When I write "every club," I mean "every club"—including your putter.

Ask the better golfers you know where they get their clubs. Most metropolitan areas have a genius tucked away in a small out-of-the-way shopping center. He will likely have some of the modern technologies that provide key raw data, but the better clubfitters will take a few measurements, watch you swing, and then make a few recommendations. You might have some ideas about certain brands that you like, and you might have tried a few "demo" clubs that you liked, but if you trust the clubfitter entirely, your chances of getting the results you want from your clubs improve dramatically. To find a clubfitter in your area, visit the Association of Golf Clubfitting Professionals' Web site (www.clubfitter.org). Your clubfitter can also recommend the type of ball you should use.

One of the joys of any hobby is going to an auction site like eBay. I have purchased and sold several clubs on eBay and have always been delighted with the result. I purchased a true professional-caliber putter through an online auction, and the putter, after my James Bond cufflinks, is my favorite possession. eBay is best for relatively hard-to-find clubs and other used items. It can also be a good way to sell used clubs. But buyer beware: stories abound of people who have purchased brand-name equipment at crazy discounts only to discover that the clubs were knockoffs—fakes. Check that the seller has a true seller rating and that the store has an actual physical location.

And finally, remember that the right grip size is important, but the most important part of the club is probably the shaft. Better players tend to use stiffer shafts because they have higher clubhead speeds. Trust your clubfitter to get you the shafts that best suit your game.

Forged vs. Cast

Irons and wedges (and putters even) come in two flavors: forged and cast. Forged irons are not fakes but are literally forged out of carbon steel. When making cast clubs, hot metal is poured into a mold. In the past decade, the difference between cast irons and forged irons has narrowed, but there are still advantages to both. Forged irons are more malleable and thus can be tweaked by a clubfitter; they also tend to look better than cast clubs. But the major benefit is feel: hitting a golf ball in the middle of the sweet spot with a forged iron is one of the best feelings in all of golf. Better golfers like forged clubs because they make it easier to work the ball, high or low, fade or draw. Cast clubs, though, offer significantly more forgiveness and a larger sweet spot than forged clubs.

Today's forged clubs offer more feel and better forgiveness than in the past. Today's cast clubs offer better feel than in the past. So forged or cast is more a case of personal preference. One of the reasons I enjoy golf is for the feel of a well-struck iron, so that's why I have always had forged clubs. But I do give up a little forgiveness on off-center hits. Plenty of high handicappers love forged clubs, and plenty of professional golfers will play with nothing except cast clubs.

THE BASIC RULES OF GOLF ETIQUETTE

- ✦ Try to play quickly at all times.
- ✦ Turn your cell phone off.
- ✦ When your playing partner is about to play, stay still and remain totally silent.

✦ The person who had the lowest score on the previous hole plays first.

✦ Do not throw clubs.

✦ The person who is farthest from the hole plays first unless the club or course allows or mandates "ready golf." Ready golf is when you play when you are ready and do not wait for the person or people who might be farthest from the hole.

✦ Take care of the golf course. Rake bunkers so that nobody can tell that anyone was there. Fix pitch marks on the green so that you would be happy to putt over what you have just repaired. Fix divots.

✦ Count every stroke.

✦ Be good company at all times.

✦ If you have been the guest of a member at a club, write a thank-you note.

WHEN TO WRITE A THANK-YOU NOTE

✦ When you have been the guest of a member at a club.

✦ When you are visiting a club and one of the professionals has been helpful.

✦ When you are experiencing success with your instructor.

An e-mail or phone call will not suffice. A hand-written note on personal stationery is the preferred choice for a thank-you note from an intelligent golfer. However, you can also type the note on business stationery—especially if the golf outing was business-related. Here is an example letter:

Dear Robert,

Many thanks for the opportunity to play Scunthorpe Hollow Country Club last week. It was a thrill to play a course that is so highly ranked in *Golf Chronicle* magazine, and I especially enjoyed the final few holes that play toward the wonderful bungalow-style clubhouse. The course was in magnificent condition.

I also enjoyed the drinks and supper afterward. All in all, it made for a great day of golf, and I hope I have a chance to reciprocate in the very near future. Thank you again for the excellent golf and company.

Sincerely,

Derek A. Clive

Derek A. Clive

Business on the Golf Course

If you are the host, the golf course is a wonderful place to spend time with current or prospective clients, especially if you are a member of a top club or have access to a top resort. If you are trying to persuade someone who is not yet a client to become one, then it's perfectly acceptable to invite that person for a round of golf, especially if you are close to securing the "deal." Your time with the prospective client should ideally begin with a light lunch, followed by thirty to forty-five minutes to warm up, followed by the golf. After the round, you might wish to include dinner at the club or at a separate location.

Before your guests arrive, you might wish to inform them of any dress code requirements at the club and ask whether they prefer to ride, walk, or take a caddy. Your No. 1 job is to make your guests feel at ease. Your second job is not to talk too much about business. Your goal during the visit should be to get to know your guests a little better and to enjoy some quiet time away from the office. Generally, the intelligent golfer avoids talking business at lunch and on the golf course, unless the guests initiate a business conversation.

If they are not serious golfers, they might be intimidated by going to a golf club, so if you are going to use the golf course for business, you must do everything you can to make them feel at ease. After the round, it is acceptable to bring up any business discussions, albeit briefly. You should not "press gang" the potential clients or have other members of your company appear out of nowhere. You can initiate the business part of the conversation with simple open-ended questions: "Do you have questions about what we have discussed in the past few weeks?" or "Is there anything that we need to be doing at this stage of the process?" If you have invited a current client, you might simply say, "We really appreciate your business, and if there's anything we can do to improve anything, let me know at any time." If your guest wants to take it from there, he or she will. A sure way to make the client or potential client feel uncomfortable is to wear your sales boots to the golf course.

Should you demolish your guest on the golf course? If your client is an average to good golfer, it's fun to enjoy a friendly game with a small wager—say a maximum of ten dollars. Opinions vary on this, and there are plenty of business people who would never beat a client but will happily beat anyone else. On the sadly all-too-rare occasions when a vendor asks me to play golf, I want a competitive match where my host is playing as hard as possible. We'll have a game based on handicaps. I would be suspicious of any vendor who "throws" the game just to try to make me feel good. And when I take clients out to play golf, I want to play as well as I can possibly play.

PLAYING THE GAME

WHEN YOU ARE A SINGLE

Yes, it's usually more fun to play with friends, but showing up at the first tee alone means that you will likely meet a new friend. When you do, be polite, mind your etiquette, help to look for lost balls in the deep rough, and play quickly; you'll soon be asked to play again with the people you just met. By showing up alone at the wide variety of courses I have played, I have met a kaleidoscope of fascinating people: a retired Air Force officer, the director of world marketing for a luxury car company, a former sports star, a retired policeman, a former professional who played in the Open Championship a few times, a welder, a restaurant owner, a well-known comedian, a submariner who fired a torpedo that sunk a battleship, a software guru, a top executive with a top bank, and many more.

Sometimes, when the course isn't busy, it's fun to play alone. If you want a challenge, play the score-card. Simply take your handicap, give yourself a shot at the corresponding holes, and play match play; it's also called a bogey competition. Let's say you have a 15 handicap. Give yourself a shot on the fifteen hardest holes, as marked on the scorecard. On those holes, you win if you have a par or better, you tie if you have a bogey, and you lose if you have a double bogey or worse. On the holes where you don't get a shot, you have to par the hole to tie, and so on. See if you can "beat the course" with your handicap.

Some courses, particularly those in England and Scotland, are strict about singles, especially when the course is typically busy. If you are a single on the first tee at a course in the United Kingdom, it's possible, even likely, that a bellicose member will yell, "A single has no standing on the course!" There is no need to panic or wrap your hybrid around the man's neck. Simply wait until the course slows down or ask the professional to pair you up with a group.

DON'T BE A COMMENTATOR

The most annoying person in golf is the commentator. After you have hit the ball into a bunker off the tee, the commentator will say, "That's in the bunker." But after you have hit a glorious shot out of the bunker to within three inches of the hole, the commentator will hit the mute button. After you have hit the ball deep in the woods, the commentator will say, "That's clearly deep in the woods, and you have no chance of finding it." When you are playing with a commentator, your best bet is to try to ignore him or her.

In response to the annoying commentator, though, do not become a commentator yourself, make any disparaging comments, or give up your standards of etiquette by coughing loudly during a putt. If you have been playing a long time and the commentator is new to the game, it's perfectly acceptable to take the person aside after the game and explain that intelligent golfers are not commentators. Still, your best bet is to ignore the commentator and avoid playing with that person ever again.

Unless you are playing with friends who don't mind a bit of jocular and mostly well-intentioned ribbing, here are the general guidelines for the intelligent golfer:

✦ When a playing partner hits a poor shot, say nothing.

✦ If the bad shot means that the ball is in deep rough or deep woods, help find the ball and take great pride in finding it.

✦ When a playing partner hits a good shot, offer congratulations, but only once the ball has come to a full stop.

✦ Be aware of a good shot hit from a particularly bad situation. If your playing partner has a poor lie in a bunker but manages to get the ball onto the putting surface, congratulate him heartily; that's a shot a professional would be proud to own.

✦ If a playing partner is having a consistently bad day, do not offer swing advice under any circumstance.

Remember: A golfer having a poor round just wants to be left alone. But a golfer having a great round will relish the kudos.

When to Concede

If you are playing a match, your opponent's ball may roll to within a few inches of the hole. At this stage, the intelligent golfer has a decision to make. Should you concede the very short putt, or should you make your opponent putt the ball to finish the hole? The concession of putts is one of the most controversial and contentious issues in all of golf. To make it less so, here are some basic guidelines for the intelligent golfer:

- ✦ The object of the game is to get the ball into the hole in the fewest possible strokes—*into*, not *near*.

- ✦ Even the very best golfers sometimes miss extremely short putts.

- ✦ You should never *ask* for a concession.

- ✦ You have no obligation to offer a concession, even if the ball is an inch from the cup.

- ✦ Your "concession threshold" is yours and yours alone.

- ✦ Never expect your opponent to give you a putt.

- ✦ If your opponent asks for a concession, there's a 99 percent chance that he or she does not like the look of the upcoming putt. Make your opponent putt the ball. But before you do, say, "I should give it to you, but I enjoy watching you putt as you have a very good stroke, so I'll let you putt." You can also say, "I think I'll take a look at that one," which means that you want your opponent to putt out.

✦ On the eighteenth green, if you are away and putting for a birdie to win the match and your opponent is five or fewer feet from the hole and putting for par, it is generally considered good form to concede that putt. If you make the birdie putt, then you have won fair and square; if you miss the birdie putt, then your opponent will likely give you your putt and you can shake hands and celebrate a hard-fought "half" or tie.

Poor putters and poor competitors ask for, or even demand, a lot of concessions. Remember that even Jack Nicklaus missed some very short putts and that a one-foot putt counts the same as a 300-yard drive right down the middle of the fairway.

BE A GOOD, IF NOT GREAT, PUTTER

Despite what the equipment manufacturers and their marketing people will have you believe, few golfers have the physical capacity to hit the ball great distances. People who can hit the ball close to 300 yards do not grow on trees. However, any intelligent golfer can become an excellent putter. There are four steps:

+ Buy a putter fitted specifically to you, and have a qualified putter fitter fit you.

+ Take putting lessons from a professional golfer who is a good putter and has had to make tough putts under pressure; that professional will understand the key mechanics.

+ Stick with your teacher's methodology, and ignore everyone else.

+ Practice your putting more than any other part of your game. If you can putt well, you will always get a game and you will always be in the game. (You will also annoy the pants off everyone you play with!)

YOUR HANDICAP

Every intelligent golfer should have an official USGA handicap. Today, calculating your handicap is easier than ever. In some instances, you can enter scores online through your club or your state or regional golf association. Many clubs have a computer located in or near the locker room where you can enter your scores as you finish a round. When you enter a score, be aware that you are supposed to lower your score if your round included some big numbers. For example, if your current handicap is 0–9, then you cannot, for handicap purposes, have a score on a hole higher than two over par. If you had a seven on a par-4, then you have to reduce it to a six before you enter your score in the handicap computer.

The formula that the USGA uses to determine handicaps would likely baffle a nuclear physicist; a full description and explanation of the system would take half this book. Essentially, your handicap represents 80 percent of your average number of shots over par; the number represents what you should shoot if you are playing your best. Every time you play a round and you count up all your strokes, you are supposed to enter your score.

Golfers have been known to enter artificially high numbers so that they can carry an inflated handicap. In the United Kingdom, such a person is called a *rogue*. Don't be a rogue. (In the United States that person is called a sandbagger.) You will be immensely unpopular if you have a 13 handicap and shoot 74 in the second flight of the club championship. People (like me) will batter you verbally throughout the round and call you a cheat, which is exactly what you are.

Some golfers enter only their better scores so that they can claim a better handicap than their skill level indicates. For example, you might play with someone who has a 5 handicap but clearly cannot break 85. It's called a "vanity handicap" for a reason.

The intelligent golfer always plays fair.

Which Tees Should You Play?

If a golf course is experiencing problems with slow play, it's probably because the starter isn't getting the golfers to play the correct set of tees. The male intelligent golfer whose handicap is 0–5 has the right to go to the back tees. If his handicap is 6–11, he should play from the next set up. If his handicap is over 11, he should play from the next set up. The female intelligent golfer should play the red tees unless she is a college golfer or one of the state's top amateurs.

When you Play Golf with a Caddy

If you belong to a club with caddies, you will likely have a favorite or regular caddy; that relationship is one to cherish and foster over the years. The caddy will get to know your game and will steer you around the golf course based on your ability.

When you visit a resort or a golf course and the caddy master assigns you a caddy, you are beginning a new relationship with a new caddy—and this can be exciting or round-wrecking, depending on where you are and your approach. Such relationships are more formal and organized at a resort, where most of the caddies will have taken a customer service program. Still, you can count on spending several hours with a true character who will not, thankfully, follow every tenet of the customer service manual.

In Scotland or Ireland, you can be *absolutely certain* that the caddies have not taken any sort of customer appreciation training. Caddies there, however, seem to have a sixth sense and can often understand your ability and handicap just by looking at you, watching you warm up on the first tee, or looking in your golf bag. Your job is simple: trust your caddy. If on a par-3 of about 130 yards, he tells you to take a 6-iron, take the 6-iron. If he tells you that a putt is a foot outside the left edge and it looks straighter than a Roman road, hit the putt a foot outside the left edge. If you fail to follow the advice of your caddy, you will likely get the cold shoulder for the rest of the round. Your caddy seriously wants to help you, partly from a desire to see that you enjoy your visit to the course. But there's an ulterior motive: cash. To keep things interesting, many caddies bet on the outcome of your game.

TIPPING

If you play golf and you visit golf clubs and resorts, as an intelligent golfer you will be expected to tip certain people certain amounts at certain times. Tipping, as in other arenas, should generally match the quality of the service. Here are some guidelines:

- ✦ **Caddy in Scotland.** Average service: £40; good service: £60; excellent service: £80. Do not pay in dollars and most certainly not in euros.

- ✦ **Caddy at Pinehurst or similar resort (in addition to the per-bag fee).** Average service: $60; good service: $80; excellent service: $100.

- ✦ **Van/bus driver in Scotland or Ireland (for the week).** One person on the bus should put together a collective tip: £30 to £50 per person.

- ✦ **Wait staff and bar staff at a resort or hotel.** Normal tipping applies; roughly 15 to 20 percent. In the United Kingdom, many restaurants and hotels include the service charge automatically.

Tipping is always totally at your discretion. No law says you have to tip or that you have to follow any guidelines. People whose compensation depends, in part, on tips, know this as well.

WALKING

The best way to enjoy golf is to walk. And the best way to enjoy the walk is with fellow walkers and a caddy. Some golf courses are only realistically playable with a cart, which is a pity. If you have the choice between a course or club that *encourages* walking and one that *discourages* walking, choose the former. Many North American clubs make the mistake of allowing golf carts but banning pull-carts or "trolleys." There is nothing wrong with a trolley. If you go to perhaps the finest and most civilized golf club in the United Kingdom—Sunningdale—you will see numerous members using trolleys of various shapes and sizes.

THE SUN

Dermatologists tell golfers to wear a hat with a wide brim, sunscreen, long pants, and shirts with long sleeves. That's all good advice, especially for those intelligent golfers who play a lot of golf in sunny climates. However, the most important piece of protective equipment is a top-quality pair of golf-specific sunglasses to prevent eye-related problems later in life.

DRINKING ON THE GOLF COURSE

Physicians will tell you that it's a good idea to stay well hydrated on the golf course, especially in hot weather. Some golfers take this advice quite literally and drink at least one can of liquid refreshment per hole—usually a beer. I have played with those individuals, and the results can range from fun and entertaining to stupid and boorish. Those who feel that there is a time and place for everything generally avoid drinking while playing golf but will enjoy something after golf. The intelligent golfer does not get drunk on the golf course. In fact, nothing could be *less* intelligent.

Many golf courses, especially those at top resorts, have beverage carts well stocked with beer and other beverages. You will enjoy the golf more if you stick to the nonalcoholic beverages.

THE MUST-READ GOLF WRITERS

BERNARD DARWIN: A fine player and a connoisseur of the game, Darwin's straightforward style is highly readable, and his work provides an excellent view of the game in the first half of the twentieth century. The best introduction to Darwin's work is *Bernard Darwin on Golf*, edited by Jeff Silverman.

HERBERT WARREN WIND: The finest American golf writer, Wind was the golf writer for *The New Yorker* (and other publications). Never short for column inches, Wind wrote epic articles primarily in the 1950s and 1960s about subjects ranging from golf course architecture and construction to Jack Nicklaus. Wind was the ghostwriter for Ben Hogan's instructional books, but the best of Wind's writings can be found in a compilation of his work, *Following Through: Writings on Golf*.

PETER DOBEREINER: As a newspaper man, Dobereiner had to get to the point, and his style often shows that edge. But in his many and varied works of nonjournalism, he struts his stuff more readily, often indulging in long sentences replete with strange and wonderful clauses. More often than not, Dobereiner wrote about the funny and tragi-comic side of golf; he was able to write about the disasters that have befallen even the best golfers without sounding mean-spirited. Every intelligent golfer should read *Golf a la Carte: The Best of Peter Dobereiner*.

ENJOYING THE GAME

ATTENDING A GOLF TOURNAMENT

If you are invited to attend a golf tournament as the guest of a friend or as part of a company outing, the person who invites you will provide you with full instructions, specifically when and where to show up. Your primary job is to enjoy yourself and enjoy the hospitality, which, at most professional golf tournaments, is usually extremely good. You will not need to wear a jacket (unless instructed), but you should wear a well-made tailored golf shirt and a pair of smart casual trousers with a pair of smart casual shoes. If the weather is going to be especially warm, your host might recommend that you wear shorts. It is totally acceptable to ask your host about the dress code for the event if you wish or if your spouse has questions. At any golf event, you cannot go wrong with the clothes you would wear if you were going to the club to play golf.

If your host has organized a corporate box or corporate tent, it is good manners to spend some time in the box or tent, but it's also perfectly fine to go out on the golf course and enjoy watching the professionals play. The next day, the intelligent golfer always writes a thank-you note to the host.

At any golf tournament, professional or otherwise, general golf etiquette rules apply. When a player is about to play a shot, remain quiet. There are two phases to a golf tournament, which usually lasts seven days. The first three days, typically, are practice rounds. For access to players, the practice days are the best; practice days are also the best for children. The players are generally relaxed and more effusive. The final four days of the tournament are more serious, and while the golf can be more entertaining when the "real bullets" are flying, the players are less accessible. The PGA Tour designates certain areas as "autograph zones," but during the practice round, it's generally acceptable to ask players for autographs. You cannot ask for autographs on non-practice round days.

At a golf tournament, you can camp at a certain hole or follow a specific player or grouping. Some people like to watch the golf at famous holes; a good alternative is to watch at a par-5 that the players can reach in two shots—you will be watching a short-game clinic that will amaze you and your group. Following a group of well-known golfers is excellent entertainment, but you will not be alone. A good alternative is to follow a group of lesser-known golfers late on a Friday afternoon as they try to make the cut. That's when you will see real pressure and some great golf, and you might well be the only person following the group.

Every golfer should attend at least one day of professional tournament golf once a year. Notice that most professional golfers play relatively quickly and they have a consistent pre-shot routine. You will also learn that even the professionals make major mistakes from time to time. You will see mostly good and excellent golf, but you will also see some bad shots. No doubt you will also notice that the professional usually follows a bad shot with a great shot.

ATTENDING A MAJOR CHAMPIONSHIP

Every golfer should attend one of the big golf tournaments at least once. There's something extra special about the major championships, and with a little advance planning (or sometimes a *lot* of advance planning), attending one of the majors is a realistic proposition. If you go just once, or even if you end up going to all of them every year (and why not?), then by all means, go in style and make the most of the opportunity.

The Masters
When Bobby Jones started the Masters in 1934, organizers were practically begging people to come. That has changed over the years, to say the least, and today, a Masters badge is one of the hottest tick-

ets in all of sports. The waiting list closed several years ago, and the chances of getting on any list for any badges are pretty much slim to none. But there is an annual lottery for practice-round tickets, and your chances of getting those are better. I'm on that list, and my name seems to pop up once every five years. Practice rounds are fun at Augusta, and just seeing the course is a delight. Visit the Web site (www.masters.org) for details.

If you absolutely have to get to the Masters during the "real thing," then your best bet is to find a golf tour specialist from the United Kingdom or Japan who has access to badges and also to luxury, or at least semi-luxurious, accommodations and dining. Just make sure that the tour operator has a good track record and will guarantee the requisite number of badges. And book early.

The U.S. Open

Tour operators and sports trip specialists sell excellent packages to attend the U.S. Open. But if you want to buy tickets and do it yourself, you must be patient—and it can help if you join the U.S. Golf Association (USGA). The first step is to visit the Web site (www.usga.org). The second step is to visit the official site of the U.S. Open (www.usopen.com).

If your company wants to sponsor a hospitality tent at the U.S. Open, these are readily available at most sites, most years; this will guarantee tickets and also provide guests and clients with a wonderful time at the most difficult championship in the world. Ticket policies for certain venues vary, so it's important to check the Web site, but one thing is always certain: USGA members get the first chance to buy tickets. As soon as you get them, if not before, book hotels and other travel; a hotel room in an above-average hotel can be very difficult to find. Remember that the USGA accepts ticket applications years ahead of each championship.

The Open Championship

Of the four majors, the Open Championship, also known as the British Open, is the easiest ticket to obtain. In most instances, you simply show up and pay the entrance fee and there is usually no limit to the number of people that can attend. Many golfers from North America wisely combine, through their tour specialist, their golf tour with a couple of days at the Open. You can, however, purchase tickets for yourself before the event. The Royal and Ancient Golf Club of St. Andrews, which organizes the Open, also offers special packages that guarantee seating at the eighteenth hole plus access to the large hospitality tent. But if you really want to go in style, book a package that also includes accommodations.

The PGA Championship

It's not the most revered of the majors, but in the past several years, it has produced some of the most exciting major championship golf. The first place to start for ticket information is the PGA's Web site (www.pga.com). You will find a link there to the upcoming championship.

The Ryder Cup

This famous match-play competition between the best professional golfers from the United States and the best professional golfers from Europe is one of the world's top sporting events and one of its toughest tickets. It's actually more of a big party than a delight for the pure golf spectator, which is to say you are not likely to see a lot of golf. Four groups go out in the morning and four go out in the afternoon for each of the first two days, and then there are twelve singles matches on the final day. Only a portion of the matches makes it all the way to the final hole. Still, it's an exciting event and a lot of fun. As with the majors, your best bet to secure a ticket plus hospitality and a luxurious place to stay is through a golf tour operator or sports event specialist. Corporate hospitality packages are also an excellent way to enjoy the Ryder Cup. For tickets, try the Web site (www.rydercup.com).

A Word about Golf Package Operators
Of the many operators in the market, most are reputable and reliable. But many are not. Understanding this, many major events will partner with an "official" package provider. This is the safest way to guarantee success.

GOLF'S GREAT
GENTLEMEN AND LADIES

Know the following, and you will learn a great deal about the most intelligent golfers.

Bobby Jones
Born and raised in Atlanta, Bobby Jones showed early promise for the game and quickly became successful in tournaments. At just eighteen years old, he qualified for the U.S. Open. While still in his twenties, he won thirteen major tournaments in just twenty attempts—all as an amateur. His most important achievement was winning all four major championships in one year. A gentleman, Jones exemplified fair play. The USGA good sportsmanship prize is called "The Bob Jones Award." Jones retired from competitive amateur golf when he was just twenty-eight to focus on his law practice and his family. He subsequently founded the Augusta National Golf Club and started a tournament

there—the Masters. Jones hosted the event and also played in the Masters until his health declined too far. Jones had syringomyelia, a painful and ultimately paralyzing disease from which he died in 1971. One of the true sports heroes of the early twentieth century, Jones helped to grow the game in numerous ways. In addition to being one of the best golfers ever to play the game, he was an excellent writer, authoring several books about golf, the best of which might be *Bobby Jones on Golf*.

Joyce Wethered

Bobby Jones once said that the best golfer he had ever seen, male or female, was Joyce Wethered, an English golfer who won several championships, including the British Women's Amateur Championship and the English Ladies' Championship. She won the former four times and the latter five. She is also known by her married name, Lady Heathcoat-Armory. Jones once played with Wethered from the back tees at the Old Course at St. Andrews. She shot 75 in a steady breeze.

Here's what Jones had to say, according to Wethered's citation in the World Golf Hall of Fame: "I have not played golf with anyone, man or woman, amateur or professional, who made me feel so utterly outclassed. It was not so much the score she made as the way she made it. It was impossible to expect that

Miss Wethered would ever miss a shot—and she never did." Like Jones, she retired from competitive golf perhaps before her peak and only played periodically in a local competition in England. Her powerful swing sent the ball about 240 yards, and it was usually struck dead straight.

Peggy Kirk Bell

Born in 1921, Bell was one of the founding members of the LPGA and toured the country promoting the tour and women's golf after World War II. With her husband, Warren "Bullet" Bell, Peggy Kirk Bell purchased Pine Needles, the iconic golf course and lodge in Southern Pines, North Carolina, just a few minutes from Pinehurst. She and her family have run Pine Needles for about half a century, and the course has hosted the U.S. Women's Open three times in the past two decades.

In addition to being a fine player, Bell is a sought-after teacher who has taught numerous good players, as well as several teachers. A trip to Pine Needles is not complete without a conversation with the gracious, charming, warm, and always elegant Mrs. Bell, who is usually in the clubhouse around dinnertime. She knows everyone and will remember your name, even if she has met you only once or twice. She has some remarkable stories to tell.

Byron Nelson

Byron Nelson was one of the most successful profes-sional golfers to play the game. In 1945, he won eleven tournaments in a row on his way to eighteen victories; he had seven second-place finishes. Nelson developed his swing just as steel shafts were beginning to replace hickory, and his swing reflected the change in equipment. Instead of using a wristy action with the hands and arms, Nelson generated power from the larger muscles of the hips and torso. At age thirty-four, he retired to a Texas ranch. He mentored many play-ers, commentated for ABC golf telecasts, and hosted an annual tournament in Dallas.

Gene Sarazen

Gene Sarazen was a small man, but he hit perhaps the most famous shot in all of golf, a double-eagle two at the par-5 fifteenth at Augusta National on his way to victory in the 1935 Masters. It is known as "the shot heard around the world." He is one of just a handful of golfers to have won all four major championships. He won seven majors and more than fifty tournaments. Sarazen played golf all over the world, mostly in exhibitions later in his career. He also hosted *Shell's Wonderful World of Golf*. At age seventy-one, on the fiftieth anniversary of his first appearance in the Open Championship, Sarazen scored a hole-in-one.

Jack Whitaker

Jack Whitaker hosted the second "season" of *Shell's Wonderful World of Golf*, and such is Whitaker's devotion to duty (and civilized dress) that he was always in a jacket and tie, even when the weather seemed volcanic. Whitaker's career has spanned several decades and several sports, although he spent much of his time in horse racing, football, and golf. If there's one golf commentator, writer, and essayist who embodies intelligent golf, it's Jack Whitaker.

Bernard Darwin

Bernard Darwin was a lawyer, writer, and excellent golfer who captained the Cambridge University golf team in 1897. He wrote about golf for *The Times* for more than forty years and also wrote for the British periodical *Country Life* for more than fifty years. Darwin was Captain of the Royal and Ancient Golf Club in 1934, perhaps golf's highest noncompetitive honor. He was around for many of the great golf moments of the first half of the twentieth century. A great stylist, he was able to describe golf courses and golfers with total clarity, as demonstrated in this excerpt about Joyce Wethered from his book *British Golf*:

> *She had fully the power of any other lady either before or after her and to that she added a deadly uniformity of accuracy only to be found among two or three of the very best men. Whatever other stars may arise one thing is certain; those who saw this truly great golfer in her prime will never admit comparisons, but will say with pardonable prejudice, "Ah, but you never saw Miss Wethered."*

Darwin poured his heart and soul into his writing, and anyone who reads his work not only will learn a great deal about the best of golf in the British Isles but will also want to get out the door and down the golf course.

The intelligent golfer follows this dictum: act as those greats have acted, and you will always be invited back.

6

DRESSING FOR THE GAME

Intelligent golfers, for the most part, have always been among the most stylish of dressers. Sometimes, admittedly, the styles have led certain golfers on bizarre tangents; the classic example must be Jack Nicklaus (and everyone else) who embraced the Sansabelt trend in the late 1970s and early 1980s. As the name implies, Sansabelt slacks were garish-looking trousers that even slightly rotund people would wear without a belt. Sansabelt is still manufacturing their product, which looks significantly better than it did several decades ago—at least on their models.

Until the late 1930s, many golfers wore ties, tweed coats, and billowing Plus Fours. In the United States, trousers that end just below the knee are sometimes called knickers. The following is a conversation that should not transpire:

SCOTTISH CADDY: Hello, sir. How are you getting on today?

AMERICAN GOLFER (wearing new knickers): Fine. Fine. Do you like my new knickers?

SCOTTISH CADDY: I don't know. I cannae see 'em, and I'm not sure I want to if you don't mind.

In the United Kingdom, "knickers" is a slightly derisive word for women's underwear. In England, Scotland, and Wales, plenty of golfers wear knickers, only they are called breeches or Plus Fours. Plus Twos are a slimline version of Plus Fours, and Plus Eights are so baggy that a brisk wind would likely carry you away. Plenty of golfers still wear, pridefully, Plus Twos or Plus Fours—and they make excellent sense for golf, especially when the course is wet and you are tramping through deep rough.

Like many other sports, golf has a uniform, or at least a dress code. Following the basics of golf dress etiquette is not difficult, nor is it necessarily draconian. And there is plenty of leeway for both men and women to express some augmented stylistic sensibility. That is to say that, on the golf course, even the intelligent golfer might go slightly bananas with color combinations, if he or she so chooses.

MEN

Shirts and Accessories

While many professionals are increasingly wearing what looks like a cross between a T-shirt and a failed attempt at a turtleneck, the mock T is not acceptable at many country clubs. In the winter, a turtleneck is acceptable, especially when worn with a sweater or sweater vest. In the summer, it is safest to wear a collared golf shirt. A wind vest or wind jacket is acceptable, as are most golf waterproofs. You will look and feel out of place if you wear a dress shirt on the golf course.

A note about logos. Since most golf shirts come with some sort of logo or emblem, you should choose your logo carefully, especially if you are visiting a club as a guest of a member. Large manufacturers' logos can seem garish, so avoid them. You should also steer clear of logos associated with sports teams or NASCAR drivers. Unless you are playing on the Hooters Tour or have a sponsorship arrangement with the restaurant chain, you should not wear a golf shirt with a Hooters logo. A shirt without a logo is fine, as is a shirt with the logo of a golf club.

Trousers/Pants/Slacks

You will be safest with a pair of khaki or blue pants, and these should be color-coordinated with your shirt. If you can organize it and if the look is somewhat tied to the other parts of your wardrobe, you can wear plaids and other colors. If you wish, you can also wear knickers, obviously with long socks that go up to the knee. With the latter, you may endure some gentle ribbing at your club, so it helps if you are an excellent golfer and can answer the retorts with a string of birdies. When visiting a club as a guest, you are generally taking a big risk if you deviate from more standard golf clothing. During warm or hot weather, shorts are acceptable at most golf courses. These should be tailored and must extend to just above the knee; if you wear shorts, do not wear long socks, unless you are playing at certain golf clubs in the United Kingdom.

Shoes

Golf courses in North America that allow traditional spikes are extremely rare. New golf shoes come with soft spikes, which are just as effective and also keep putting surfaces free of spike marks. In the winter, basic black shoes are acceptable. In the summer, basic white shoes with subtle variations are also acceptable. On men, colorful shoes are also fine, but once again, be aware of the color combinations. The intelligent golfer generally avoids wearing black shoes with shorts in the summer.

If you are confused about golf clothing, it's tempting to look at the golfers on the PGA Tour and say, "I want to dress like that." This can be risky since professional golfers have contracts with clothing companies and there's often a conspiracy to get a touch garish just to get more attention. The golf professional at your club can always provide advice. If in doubt, know this: the intelligent golfer can go anywhere wearing a white shirt with an acceptable golf logo; a blue, red, or green sweater; navy-blue trousers; and black shoes.

Your grooming should be neat and tidy in general. In sunny and warm or even hot weather, a hat is a good idea. If you wear a baseball-style cap, it should be clean and should have a golf logo; golf stores have a good stock of acceptable baseball-style caps. A baseball cap with a message saying something like "Gone fishin'" is not at all acceptable for the intelligent golfer. Certain hats with wide brims are also acceptable for men as long as the hat is not too feminine. A golf visor is acceptable.

LADIES

In general, ladies who follow the guidelines above will be safe and feel comfortable. But in the past decade, women's golf clothes have become increasingly fashionable, as anyone who watches LPGA tour golf will attest. However, certain clubs, especially older, suburban clubs, might not deem certain women's golf clothing acceptable, which is understandable, especially when a golf top is short enough to reveal a pierced belly button on the follow-through.

Ladies are typically more in tune with color coordination than men and can be relied upon to wear outfits that actually match. A number of prominent golf clothing manufacturers produce exquisite clothes for women.

For men and women, following the basic guidelines will keep the intelligent golfer out of hot water. But golf provides plenty of room for stylistic elasticity. While certain items like jeans, halter tops, and frayed T-shirts are not acceptable, well-made, colorful clothing, as long as it is coordinated, is acceptable and enjoyable. Dressing up for golf can be a lot of fun and should certainly be encouraged.

AFTER GOLF

Golf clubs and resorts vary when it comes to dress guidelines inside the resort or clubhouse. Some are formal and require a jacket, dress shirt, and tie, while in others, you can wear what you wore on the golf course. To be safe, if you think that a visit to a golf club or resort will mean entering a more formal area, pack the following: a tweed jacket or blue blazer, a pressed and clean dress shirt, a tie, a clean pair of dress pants, and black or brown shoes (shined).

$$\binom{7}{}$$

DEALING WITH
GOLF DISASTERS

A lot can go right in golf, but a lot can go wrong. The former rarely gets any attention, but the latter can lead to serious consternation, bad language, and ultimately, after the passage of several months, good dinnertime storytelling and plenty of hearty belly laughs. Though very little is certain in the golf world, it's totally certain that some type of golf disaster will happen to you, usually at the time you least expect it. It's not a question of if, but when; and how, as an intelligent golfer, you deal with the disaster is a measure of your enjoyment of the game and your understanding of the subtle nuances of golf etiquette.

Disaster: You have a bad day and run out of golf balls on the thirteenth hole.

    Acceptable Reaction: Politely ask a playing partner for some extras. Do everything you can to keep those balls in play. At the end of the round, go to the golf shop and buy a dozen of the type of ball that your playing partner uses. Do not return the ones your playing partner gave you. Later that day, organize golf lessons, and next time bring more golf balls.

Disaster: You walk in your playing partner's line on the green.

Acceptable Reaction: Say, "I'm sorry, Jack; I just realized I walked in your line." Then concede the putt.

Disaster: You invite a guest to your club, and he or she proceeds to use a cell phone early and often.

Acceptable Reaction: You might want to pry the phone or device from your guest's clutches and hurl the offending device into orbit. But resist this temptation. Instead, after your guest has finished the call, ask him or her politely to turn it off. Most clubs have strict policies regarding the use of electronic devices on the golf course.

Some troubleshooting is often in order before you invite a guest, for it's often a mistake to think that your guests will automatically know your club policies. When you issue the invitation, you may wish to say something like, "Dennis, it's going to be great to see you at Lavender Hills on Tuesday. Our tee time is 2:10. You might want to know that the club is pretty strict about the dress code and also prohibits the use of cell phones and similar devices. That's just the way it is at the club. If you have any questions, feel free to ask, or there's a page on the club's Web site that has all the information."

Disaster: Something comes up, and you have to cancel your round.

Acceptable Reaction: Call your playing partners and let them know. If they cannot play either, call the golf shop and let them know that you will not be there. Few things anger a golf professional more than golfers not showing up for a tee time without calling to cancel.

Disaster: Your girlfriend or wife says that she wants to play golf with you but has never played before. And she wants to play with you today.

Acceptable Reaction: This is a potentially tricky situation but not necessarily a disaster. Your first reaction should be one of joy. Men with girlfriends or wives who play and enjoy the game are fortunate. However, you must explain that she will have to take lessons and attend some clinics before she can play at a busy time on the golf course. Explain that you will be happy to organize lessons and beginner's clinics and that you will take her out to the golf course frequently when it's less crowded. If you get a tantrum or other negative reaction, it's not your fault. Go to the golf course, and spend some extra time warming up.

Disaster: You get stuck behind the slowest group on the face of the planet, and they are not letting you through.

Acceptable Reaction: If the club or resort has a marshal, the marshal may recognize the problem and seek to sort it out. Do not call the golf shop with your cell phone; this is not a medical emergency. If you see the marshal, politely inform him or her of the problem. The intelligent golfer does not yell at the group in front, wave his arms wildly, or hit into them. If the course does not have a marshal, stop in the golf shop, if possible, after nine holes and politely and quietly let the professional know that a group is holding up play. Unfortunately, in some instances, there is just nothing you can do.

Disaster: You discover, on the first green, that you do not have a pitch mark repair tool.

Acceptable Reaction: Ask your playing partners if they have a spare one. Do this before resorting to using a tee, which is a generally poor tool for fixing a pitch mark.

Disaster: You are playing on a wet golf course and discover that the ball is muddy even though it's in the fairway.

Acceptable Reaction: Unless the club or resort has indicated at the beginning of the round that you can "lift, clean, and place" the ball, play the ball as it lies.

Disaster: You hit a wonderful drive, and the ball ends up in a divot.

Acceptable Reaction: Play the ball as it lies.

Disaster: Your playing partners start using lines from *Caddyshack*, and you feel left out because you haven't seen the movie.

Acceptable Reaction: Buy the DVD and watch the movie twenty-five times in fifty days.

Disaster: While addressing the ball, you think that you may have accidentally touched it even though it may not have moved or even oscillated.

Acceptable Reaction: Count what happened as a stroke.

Disaster: You left your golf cart and got to your ball in the fairway only to discover that you have a 5-iron when what you really need is a 7-iron.

   Acceptable Reaction: Do not go back to the golf cart. "Choke down" on the club and hit the shot. Next time, take two or three clubs with you or, better still, walk the course.

Disaster: You are playing with someone you know or don't know, and that person is a smoker who tosses cigarette butts on the ground.

   Acceptable Reaction: Quietly say, away from the others in your group, "I respectfully ask that you respect the golf course and the hard-working people who look after it; please dispose of your cigarette butts properly."

Disaster: You are playing a serious (or even not-so-serious) match, and you are unsure of a rule or a ruling.

   Acceptable Reaction: Give your opponent the benefit of the doubt, but never give yourself the benefit of the doubt.

Disaster: You are playing with some people you know but have not necessarily played golf with yet. At the beginning of the round, you agree to what you think is a low-stakes friendly wager just to keep the game interesting. At about the fourteenth tee, you realize that you and your partner are down hundreds of dollars and the most you have ever played for is around two dollars.

Acceptable Reaction: Play your best golf from this point on! If you lose, pay up. In the future, pay close attention to the stakes and the handicaps, and decline to get involved if you are not a big gambler.

Disaster: You miss the fairway from the tee and get to your ball to discover that it's very close to the out-of-bounds stakes, which are white. Upon further inspection, you discover that the ball is right on the line.

Acceptable Reaction: If you are playing a match, double-check with your opponent. In golf, the ball must be *totally* over the line to be out of bounds. But remember that the line extends from the interior of the stakes and that the line itself is out of bounds.

Disaster: Nature calls and you are nowhere near the official rest stop.

Acceptable Reaction: Nature is nature; if you can postpone the inevitable, all the better. But many courses are not blessed with a surfeit of appropriate facilities, so you might have to go to "Plan B." In this case, simply do everything you can to find a spot that is well out of view— although this can be particularly difficult at a course ringed with homes.

Everyone breaks the rules of golf etiquette from time to time—usually mistakenly, unwittingly, or out of nascent ignorance. The intelligent golfer understands this and does not get too haughty or highminded about such lapses since such an attitude would undoubtedly detract from the enjoyment of the game.

GOLF DECADENCE

Like yachting, polo, deep-sea fishing, and skiing, golf offers numerous opportunities for mega-splurges and major indulgences. Here are just a few:

Personally forged handmade irons from MacGregor Golf. The program is called Custom Grind, and you get forged professional-caliber irons made just for you and you alone. If you want the full effect, you need to visit the factory in Albany, Georgia, for your fitting session.

A golf tour of Scotland—by boat. All the best courses in Scotland and Ireland are by the sea. Right? So that means that the best way to see the best of the best is by luxury boat. Right? That's the theory behind Kalos Golf's tours, which take the intelligent golfer to the best links courses by boat. If you're a landlubber, several golf tour specialists offer helicopter shuttle service between courses.

Golf at Wynn Las Vegas. First, Steve Wynn built the most audacious golf course not just in Las Vegas but in the world. It was called Shadow Creek. When Wynn opened his new hotel and casino, Wynn Las Vegas, he decided to build his golf course literally next door on the site of the famous Desert Inn. The first tee? It's right next to the hotel.

Golf lessons with Mitchell Spearman. A *Golf Magazine* Top 100 teacher and *Golf Digest* Top 50 Teacher, Spearman has taught several of the world's top golfers, including Nick Faldo. Operating out of Manhattan Woods Golf Club in Nyack, New York, Spearman is one of the world's most expensive teachers, charging upwards of $600 an hour. But his book is always full—the first sign of a teacher who is getting results.

Private dining. The latest and trendiest resort activity is booking a private dining room and having the chef cook a meal specifically for you and your guests—usually eight to ten people. Most of the major resorts offer this new service.

The ultimate Ryder Cup package. Several golf tour specialists offer Ryder Cup packages that offer the very best in everything, including reserved box seats right next to the eighteenth green. Hotels, restaurants, and everything are top-of-the-line so that you get to see the ultimate sports event in incredible luxury and comfort.

FootJoy "My Joy" golf shoes. What about a personalized pair of golf shoes just for you? You can order pretty much any color combination and even get sports logos on your shoes if you feel so moved. The shoes arrive about three weeks after you place the order, fresh from the factory.

A Bettinardi Prototype putter. Robert Bettinardi has made putters for a number of manufacturers and currently makes them for Mizuno. Bettinardi made a number of "Tour Prototype" putters mostly for professional golfers or collectors. These exquisitely made putters come from a single block of double-aged stainless steel; most also have a honeycomb pattern on the face for the truest roll possible. If you want one, look on eBay or visit www.tksputters.com. I take my putting very seriously, and I have a Bettinardi Prototype; it's like a surgical implement.

The Confidential Guide to Golf Courses. Tom Doak, golf course architect and critic, originally wrote a book for a few friends in the business. It contained raw and unabridged reviews of the hundreds of courses around the world that Doak visited as part of his education. In the early 1990s, a publisher sanitized the original version and produced a coffee table book. The book is out of print now and costs hundreds of dollars—if you can find one. Why? Doak tells it like it is, much to the chagrin of his fellow golf course architects.

A spot in a Pro Am. Before a professional golf tournament begins, there's usually a Pro Am that benefits the tournament's chosen charity. This presents the opportunity to play with a touring professional golfer—quite a treat. And yes, people will be watching you play. The entry fee goes to charity.

GOLFERS
AND THEIR FAVORITES

TIGER WOOD's favorite movie: *Caddyshack*.

JACK NICKLAUS has taken his favorites to another level. Bear's Best is a Jack Nicklaus-designed public golf course north of Atlanta that provides golfers with the opportunity to play eighteen of his favorite golf holes. Among the choices: Cabo del Sol, Castle Pines, PGA West. There's a sister course in Las Vegas with the same theme.

ARNOLD PALMER's favorite beverage: half iced tea, half lemonade. It's called an "Arnold Palmer."

TIGER WOODS's favorite golf course: The Old Course at St. Andrews.

ERNIE ELS's favorite golf course (in Florida): Copperhead at the Westin Innisbrook Resort.

PHIL MICKELSON's favorite golf course: The Old Course at St. Andrews.

VIJAY SINGH's favorite golf course: Ballybunion.

EPILOGUE

This book serves merely as an introduction to the greatest of games. Much of the joy of golf takes place well away from the golf course and involves discovering new places, new writers, and, most important, new friends. The intelligent golfer can play golf into his nineties, if he makes it that far, and he will be constantly learning.

No book can cover all of golf; had another writer taken on this book, he or she may well have chosen a totally different set of courses, resorts, and clubs, and may have had a slightly different approach to some of the unwritten rules of etiquette and decorum. Nobody has all the answers. But I firmly believe that every intelligent golfer has five major responsibilities:

1. Enjoy every hole of every round, and try to play at least once a week.

2. Play true links golf in Scotland or Ireland at least once.

3. Find a way to help grow the game.

4. Mentor a junior golfer.

5. Fix pitch marks and help the superintendent in any way possible.

I hope that you, having read this book, enjoy this great game even more.

BIBLIOGRAPHY

Allen, Sir Peter. *The Sunley Book of Royal Golf*.
London: Stanley Paul, 1989.

Bamberger, Michael. *To the Linksland*. New York:
Penguin, 1992.

Barr, Jeff, ed. *1001 Golf Holes You Must Play Before
You Die*. Portland, ME: Ronnie Sellers Produc-
tions, 2005.

Cornish, Geoffrey, and Ronald Whitten. *The
Architects of Golf*. New York: HarperCollins,
1993.

Doak, Tom. *The Confidential Guide to Golf Courses*.
Chelsea, MI: Sleeping Bear Press, 1996.

Dobereiner, Peter. *The Book of Golf Disasters*. New
York: Perennial Library, 1983.

Dobereiner, Peter. *Golf Rules Explained*. 11th ed.
Cincinnati: David and Charles, 2005.

Lawrenson, Derek, ed. *The* Sunday Telegraph *Golf Course Guide to Britain and Ireland.* 14th ed. London: Collins Willow, 2000.

McCallen, Brian. *Golf Resorts of the World.* New York: Harry N. Abrams, 1993.

Penick, Harvey. *The Game of a Lifetime.* New York: Fireside, 1996.

Penick, Harvey. *Harvey Penick's Little Red Book.* New York: Fireside, 1999.

Rader, Dana. *Rock Solid Golf.* Charlotte: Walkabout Press, 2003.

Rubenstein, Lorne, and Jeff Neuman. *A Disorderly Compendium of Golf.* New York: Workman, 2006.

Rubenstein, Lorne. *A Season in Dornoch.* New York: Simon and Schuster, 2001.

ABOUT THE AUTHOR

Born in Hyde Park, Cincinnati, Scott Martin spent his formative years in Montreal and then London, where he attended Harrow School. He returned to the United States to attend the University of North Carolina, where he was a Morehead Scholar. In 1988, he graduated with a degree from the department of Comparative Literature, now part of the English curriculum.

Martin has contributed to numerous golf and nongolf publications and has worked on more than fifteen books as an author, editor, or compiler, including the *Insiders' Guide to Golf in the Carolinas* and *The Book of Caddyshack: Everything You Ever Wanted to Know About the Greatest Movie Ever Made*. He has worked on projects with noted golf instructors Dana Rader, Jim McClean, Robert Baker, and Mitchell Spearman. Golf has taken him to many of the world's great golf destinations, including the

Kintyre Peninsula in western Scotland, where he is a member of the Machrihanish Golf Club.

As part of a concurrent career in custom and niche publishing, Martin has created and operated several publications and is currently the publisher of *Ballantyne Magazine* in Charlotte, where he plays golf to a 7 handicap (sometimes). Today, Martin's writing focuses primarily on books, manuals, and direct response copy. He can be reached through his Web site, www.scottmartincreative.com.